Helmut Reisener

Englisch üben für den Hauptschulabschluss

MANZ VERLAG

Manz Verlag
© Ernst Klett Verlag GmbH, Stuttgart 2002
Alle Rechte vorbehalten
Muttersprachliche Beratung: Mary Ratcliffe, München
Lektorat: Harald Kotlarz, Rottenburg
Umschlaggestaltung: Zembsch' Werkstatt, München
Illustration: Sven Palmowski, Stuttgart
Druck: Ludwig Auer GmbH, Donauwörth
Printed in Germany

ISBN 3-7863-2120-5

Tipps zum Training mit diesem Buch

Wenn du dich auf einen guten Abschluss der Hauptschule im Fach Englisch vorbereiten möchtest, dann findest du hier alles, was du dafür brauchst. Vier Themenbereiche kannst du in diesem Buch trainieren:

A   Wortschatz
B   Grammatik
C   Texte
D   Tests (Original Abschlussprüfungen für den Qualifizierten Hauptschulabschluss in Bayern)

Und zu allen Übungen findest du im hinteren Teil des Buches die Lösungen.

Wie gehst du am besten vor?

● Schau in deine Hefte oder frage deine Lehrerin oder deinen Lehrer, wo du die meisten Fehler machst. Dann schlage die Seite zum Inhalt auf und suche dir das entsprechende Kapitel heraus. Du kannst jedes Kapitel unabhängig von den anderen angehen, du musst das Buch also nicht von vorn bis hinten durcharbeiten.

● Willst du aber umfassend trainieren, dann kannst du auch alle Kapitel durchgehen. Die Übungen sind überschaubar lang und du findest in den Tipps auch praktische Hilfen, wie du am besten vorgehen kannst. Außerdem gibt es auch einige Übungen, die nicht so ganz ernst gemeint sind. Etwas zum Lachen zwischendurch kann nicht schaden.

● Bevor du dich aber in eine Übung hineinstürzt, solltest du dir die Beispiele anschauen und die Erklärungen durchlesen. Ein kleiner Vitamintrunk an der Merk-Bar wird dir sicherlich auf die Sprünge helfen, da stehen nämlich die wichtigsten Regeln kurz und klar.

● Erst wenn du mit einer Übung fertig bist, solltest du im Lösungsteil nachschauen. So kannst du dich selbst kontrollieren und feststellen, dass du immer besser wirst.

● Mit diesem Zeichen Q haben wir Übungen kenntlich gemacht, die speziell für Schülerinnen und Schüler gedacht sind, die sich auf den Quali vorbereiten möchten oder müssen.

Viel Erfolg und eine gute Englischnote!

Inhalt

A *Workshop Words*

1 Laute – Buchstaben – Wörter

In diesem Workshop erfährst du Wissenswertes über die Beziehungen zwischen Wort und Laut. Das ist ganz nützlich, weil du so herausfinden kannst, wie ein Wort geschrieben wird, das du gehört hast. Und natürlich auch umgekehrt. Außerdem lernst du auch einige Tricks, wie man Wörter bilden kann.

> *Do you think that school is cool – or would you say that school is cruel?*

cruel: grausam

Wenn wir uns diese Frage anschauen und anhören, dann sehen wir sofort, dass man bei dem Verhältnis von Buchstaben und Lauten ganz schön auf der Hut sein muss:

Der Laut [u:] wird hier zum Beispiel auf vier verschiedene Weisen geschrieben:

| do – you – school / cool – cruel |

Denkt man nun noch an *shoe, two, ruler* und *new,* dann ist erst einmal Sammeln und Sortieren angesagt.

1. Wie viele Reimwörter mit [u:] schaffst du?

blue, _____   school, tool   tool: Werkzeug

_____ [u:] _____

fruit, _____   spoon   spoon: Löffel

_____ _____

knew

_____

5

2. In jeder Reihe findest du **drei Reimwörter**. Kreise sie ein.

a) [uː]   team – two – toy – too – through – tower – toast

b) [ɔː]   star – fine – four – drive – go – store – window – door

c) [iː]   sit – sea – set – friend – sky – street – key – me

d) [əʊ]   earth – dog – goes – fresh – nose – down – grows – tooth

e) [ɜː]   flat – bird – event – heard – floor – word – flag – frog

tooth: Zahn

event: Ereignis
frog: Frosch

Schauen wir nun noch einmal auf die Kapitelüberschrift und auf die Frage in der Sprechblase zurück:

Wenn du das alles (halblaut) liest, dann merkst du, dass die Buchstabenverbindung *or* in *words* anders klingt als bei dem Wort *or*. Im Britischen Englisch (BE) gibt es das nicht hörbare **r**. Beim Schreiben kann man es darum leicht vergessen.

3. Hier haben wir zwei Beispielgruppen, bei denen du vielleicht noch etwas auffüllen kannst:

shore: Ufer,
Küste

learn _____   *shore,* _____   *for,* _____

surf, _____

_____ **[ɜː]** _____   _____ **[ɔː]** _____

serve: dienen

serve _____   *girl* _____   *four* _____

_____

4. Finde nun weitere Geschwister für die folgenden Lautfamilien.

site: Standort

a) flight, sight, site, *write, right,* _____

claim: Anspruch

b) name, same, claim, _____

c) sport, short, brought, _____

ghost: Gespenst

d) coast, most, ghost, _____

e) try, buy, eye, _____

f) sound, round, _____

Can you see the sea?

No, but I can hear it from here!

Tipp

Achten muss man (beim Lesen ebenso wie beim Schreiben) vor allem auf die stummen Buchstaben.

5. STUMM, aber nicht sprachlos.

In der ersten Reihe wird in jedem Wort <u>ein</u> Buchstabe <u>nicht</u> gesprochen. Markiere ihn mit einem Stift.
In der zweiten Reihe sind es dann jeweils <u>zwei</u> oder <u>drei</u> Buchstaben, die du nicht als Laute hörst. Kreise auch diese ein.

a) nose – goes – hello – what – two – toast – blue – eleven – twelve

b) write – right – through – caught – brought – receipt – skateboard

receipt:
Empfang,
Quittung

6. Schreibe diese kurze („dramatische") Geschichte in normalem Englisch auf.

My little sister K8 *My little sister Kate* _____

said "Come on, m8, _____

lets's sk8!" _____

She didn't want to w8, _____

ran str8 up to the g8 _____

and didn't concentr8 _____

and then it was too l8. _____

Dear me, that's what I h8! _____

_____

7. Ein Lautbild – Zwei Wörter

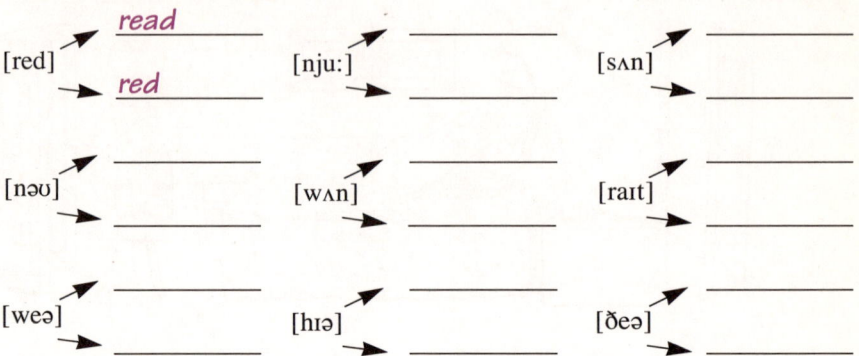

[red] → *read*
[red] → *red*

[njuː] →
[njuː] →

[sʌn] →
[sʌn] →

[nəʊ] →
[nəʊ] →

[wʌn] →
[wʌn] →

[raɪt] →
[raɪt] →

[weə] →
[weə] →

[hɪə] →
[hɪə] →

[ðeə] →
[ðeə] →

8. Lautfamilien. Finde weitere Wörter mit dem jeweiligen Laut.

[əʊ]: go, show, *blow*, _____

[aɪ]: blind, buy, my, _____

[aʊ]: sound, cow, _____

[ɔɪ]: boy, avoid, _____

[eɪ]: date, rain, _____

[ɪə]: ear, here, hear, _____

[eə]: there, fare, _____

[ʊə]: tour, sure, _____

9. *e-devils at work*
Hier haben die *e-devils* ihr Unwesen getrieben.
Kannst du korrigieren?

havn and hll ● coff and ta
● a casstt with poms
● that's intrsting ● a bottl of br
● for hr or for m ?
● W hav got an -mail

8

heaven and hell _____

_____

_____

_____

_____

10. Der Buchstabe **e**

Im Deutschen ist **e** der meistgebrauchte Buchstabe. Wusstest du das?
Auch im Englischen kommt das **e** in sehr vielen Wörtern vor. Dummer-
weise hört man aber nicht immer ein **e**. Setz die Wörter in die richtige
Liste. Aber sprich sie dir erst einmal halblaut vor.

[–]:   Nicht als Laut wahrzunehmen:

home _____

_____

_____

[e]:   Als [e]-Laut wahrzunehmen:

them _____

_____

_____

[i:]: Allein oder verdoppelt als [i:]-Laut
wahrzunehmen:

me _____

_____

_____

dress feet
we   tomatoes
home   get
them   canoe
blue   me tree pet he
shoe   when
nice   sheep
middle then
teeth leg she

11. Noch mehr Zahlen- und Buchstabenspaß gefällig?

a) I C U 2 4 T . _I see you two for tea._

b) I h8 2 B Cn . _____

c) Could U w8 4 me? _____

d) O me 10der, O me true. (Elvis Presley song): _Love_ _____

_____

e) Who R U w8ing 4 ? _____

f) A man to the tank of his car: R U M T ? _____

_____

12. Wörter mit **y**
Auch der Buchstabe **y** hat es in sich. Ergänze bei allen Wörtern das
y am Ende und ordne sie in die entsprechenden Lautgruppen ein.

~~pla~~   da   ~~lad~~   craz   sill   ver

alread   ma   **-y**   cit   bus   wh

sa   tr   identit   identif   bod   bu

simplif   m

[ɪ]	[eɪ]	[aɪ]
lady	_play_	_identify_
_____	_____	_____
_____	_____	_____
_____	_____	_____
_____	_____	_____

13. *A fable*

Und nun eine Geschichte: Die alte Fabel vom Löwen und der Maus. Allerdings hat der Computer hier ein Chaos verursacht: Der Buchstabe **O** fehlt. Schreibe den Text bitte richtig auf.

ne mrning a lin wh was hungry and wh was lking fr fd in the wds almst stepped n a muse. "Please, Mr Lin," cried the muse, "dn't eat me. I'd nly be a very small meal fr yu!" – "Yu are right," said the lin, and he carefully stepped arund the little animal.

Later the same day the muse saw the lin again. But nw the lin was a prisner in a net which sme lin-hunters had hidden in the wds. With his sharp little teeth the muse gnawed thrugh the net, and the lin was free. "Hw can I thank yu, little friend?" the lin asked. "Never mind," the muse answered. "Yu let me g free earlier tday, s it was my turn t let yu g free.

gnawed: nagte

Schreibe in dein Heft oder auf einem Blatt. So fängt es an:

One morning a lion who was hungry...

Du kannst den (verbesserten) Text für ein Partnerdiktat nutzen.

14. *Double trouble*

So ein Computer ist schon ein wertvoller Helfer (jedenfalls, wenn er funktioniert). Bei diesem Textverarbeitungsprogramm gab es leider Probleme: Es wurden keine Doppelbuchstaben erkannt. Darum musst du wieder ran und die fehlenden Buchstaben ergänzen.

a terible tothache – *a terrible toothache*

toothache: Zahnschmerzen

fod for fitnes –

grany's god glases –

boring scholboks –

buter and cotage chese –

a feling for fotbal –

a sily rabit –

Übrigens: double trouble sagt man in England auch für „Zwillinge".

a hand-writen leter –

15. Anlaut **-s**

Die Sache mit dem angehängten -s kennst du von der Pluralbildung her, aber auch bei den Verben mit *he, she, it* im *simple present.* Nun machen wir es einmal anders und setzen das **S** bei den folgenden Wörtern an den Anfang. Was kommen dabei für neue Wörter heraus? Vorsicht mit der Aussprache! Wenn du einige noch nicht kennst, schlage sie nach.

mile *smile*_____   hut _____   in _____   team _____

top _____   it _____   on _____   pill _____

hop _____   cream _____   tall _____   low _____

tart _____   eat _____   tick _____   old _____

and _____   end _____   how _____   hell _____

2   Singular und Plural

1. Ergänze den Plural.

Die meisten Substantive bilden ihren **Plural (Mehrzahl)**, indem ein -s angehängt wird. Es gibt aber auch einige Substantive, bei denen musst du -es anhängen oder aus einem -y ein -ie machen. Manchmal ändern sich auch nur einige Buchstaben, wie bei *foot – feet*.

voice: Stimme

a) voice *voices*_____   h) woman _____   o) teacher _____

b) child _____   i) bus _____   p) foot _____

c) man _____   j) glass _____   q) thief _____

sheep: Schaf

d) boy _____   k) wife _____   r) sheep _____

goose: Gans

e) tooth _____   l) tomato _____   s) goose _____

f) country _____   m) rule _____   t) fish _____

potato: Kartoffel

g) potato _____   n) language _____

2. Singular- und Pluralformen
Welche der folgenden Substantive haben keine Singularform, keine Pluralform, beides, also eine Plural- und eine Singularform?

> trousers homework actress
>
> path information sunshine coffee sunglasses
>
> child money oil mouse Biology Physics
>
> jeans house woman wildlife salt stuntman
>
> quiz sports electricity Mathematics tomato
>
> clothes pyjamas boy scissors rain train butter

actress: Schauspielerin

scissors: Schere

Trage ein:

keine Pluralform	keine Singularform	beide Formen
homework	trousers	actress/actresses

3. Schreibe diese Geheimnachrichten auf.

a) Y R U :–O ? *Why are you sad?*

b) C U l8er, allig8or _____

c) Thank U 4 not Q. _____

d) Don't :–(, B :–) (song) _____

e) R U :–)) ? _____

f) An I 4 an I, a 2th 4 a 2th (the Bible): _____

3 Wortbildung

1. Wortbildung ist vielfach eine Sache der Endungen. Die folgenden Wörter mit diesen Endungen sagen dir, wo Menschen herkommen oder was sie tun. Vervollständige die Wörter mit der passenden Endung und schreibe sie in die entsprechende Spalte.

manag- doct- Canad- post- chem- tour- settl- Ind- music- advis- police- Egypt- cycl- farm- offic- direct- fire- visit- optim- operat- art- fisher- camera- act- ectric-

-er	-or	-ist	-ian	-man/-woman
		chemist		

Schau in einem Wörterbuch nach, wenn du dir bei einem Wort nicht sicher bist.

2. Hauptwörter – Substantive – *nouns*
Alles das Gleiche, nur hat es verschiedene Namen. Mit einigen
Endungen kanst du im Englischen ganz bequem Substantive bilden.
Versuch es mit diesen besonders häufigen Endungen.

-ness   *happiness, fitness,* _____

_____

-ing   *meaning, shopping, opening,* _____

_____

-ment   *government, entertainment, equipment,* _____

_____

-(t)ion   *connection, competition, communication,* _____

_____

_____

-(t) y   *safety, responsibility,* _____

_____

_____

Wenn dir keine Wörter einfallen sollten, dann schau in das Vokabelverzeichnis am Ende deines Lehrbuchs. Experten können auch zu
einem Wörterbuch greifen.

Tipp

3. Vorsilben + Nachsilben
Trage die richtigen Adjektive ein, die du von den folgenden Verben
ableiten musst.

You can eat (do) it, so it's *eatable* _____

a) eat

You can't eat (do) it, so it's *uneatable* _____

. . . can do it . . . _____

b) drink

. . . can't do it . . . _____

. . . can . . . _____

c) forget

. . . can't . . . _____

. . . can . . . _____

d) read

. . . can't . . . _____

. . . can . . . _____

e) wash

. . . can't . . . _____

. . . can . . . _____

*accept: anneh-
men, akzeptie-
ren*

f) accept

. . . can't . . . _____

4 Hilfreiche Abkürzungen

1. In der Kürze liegt die Würze.
Hier nun wieder etwas sehr Nützliches, das zugleich auch noch Spaß macht. Abkürzungen erkennen und nutzen ist hilfreich und spart Zeit. Kannst du richtig zuordnen?

r) kilometre(s)   g) ~~television~~   a) foot/feet

1	TV
2	PC
3	USA
4	GB
5	Mr
6	£
7	m
8	CD-ROM
9	L. A.

d) Frau   n) vormittags

q) miles per hour/Meilen pro Stunde

k) Compact Disk-Read Only Memory

b) New York

10	a. m.
11	Mrs
12	NASA
13	$
14	NY
15	p. m.
16	ft
17	mph
18	km

p) nachmittags   h) personal computer

f) United States of America   j) mile(s)   e) pound (Pfund)

c) National Aeronautics and Space Administration   o) dollar

i) Herr   m) Los Angeles   l) Great Britain

1	2	3	4	5	6	7	8	9	10	11	12	13	14	15	16	17	18
g)																	

2. **Nicht ganz so ernst gemeinte Abkürzungen**

a) Finde die Lösungen!

> T = ty   M = em   P = py   D = dy
>
> G = gy   B = by

boD _____   NovMber _____   noboD _____

ciT _____   SeptMber _____   baB _____

nasT _____   DecMber _____   BioloG _____

empT _____   grumP _____   enerG _____

identiT _____   technoloG _____   poverT _____

b) Überlege dir selbst noch weitere Beispiele und verschlüssele sie.

_____

_____

_____

_____

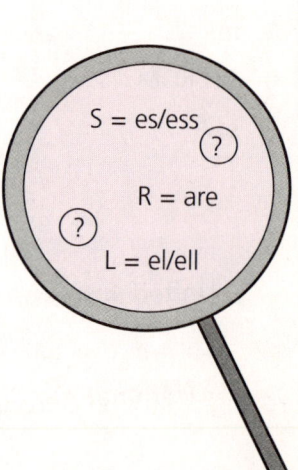

S = es/ess ?

R = are

? L = el/ell

5   Präpositionen

Oben, unten, entlang, dazwischen, davor … viele kleine
Wörter, ohne die du aber nicht sagen kannst, was du
eigentlich meinst. Im Englischen ist es genauso. Schau
die Zeichnungen an, dann weißt du, wie es funktioniert. Und dann ab zum Training.

1.   Schreib drei Sätze zu dem Bild. Die hier verwendeten Präpositionen
geben an, wo sich etwas oder jemand befindet.

A man is standing by the window.

_____

_____

_____

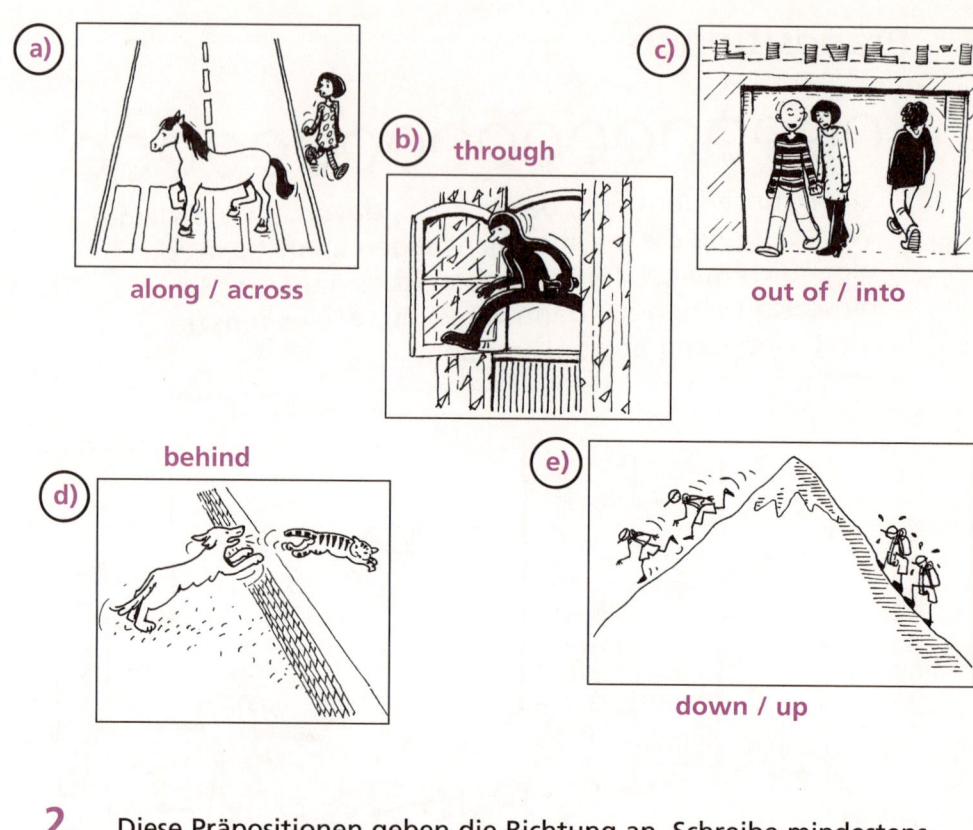

a) along / across

b) through

c) out of / into

d) behind

e) down / up

2. Diese Präpositionen geben die Richtung an. Schreibe mindestens einen Satz zu jedem Bild.

a) *The girl is walking along the road.*

b) _____

c) _____

d) _____

e) _____

_____

3. **Diese Sätze haben alles bis auf die Präpositionen. Setze sie ein.**

a) Let's look _____ this wonderful picture. – b) She's _____ London.

c) We'll leave the train _____ Liverpool Street Station. – d) The headmaster

is talking _____ the new boy. – e) Riding _____ the hill with your bike is

good for you. f) Is there a computer shop _____ here? – g) We walked

_____ Oxford Street. – h) Look, this silly boy is hiding _____ a

hide: verstecken
silly: dumm

tree.

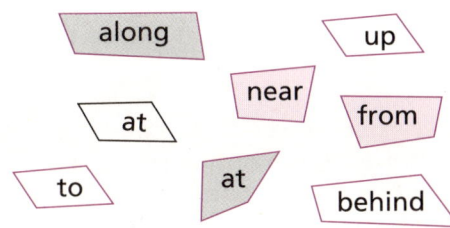

4. **Fragen über Fragen. Setze die passende Präposition ein, du findest**
sie verschlüsselt in der Box.

a) Where is she _____ ? – b) Who are you waiting _____ ? –

c) I didn't understand them. What were they talking _____?

d) Which animal is Paul afraid _____ ? – e) What are you looking

_____ ? – f) You are visiting your friends next month. Who do you

stay _____ ?

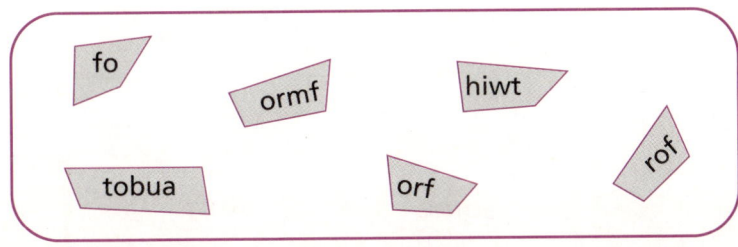

Dir ist bestimmt aufgefallen, dass die Präposition bei W-Fragen (mit
who, where, what) gern ans Ende des Satzes wandert.

Tipp

6 *Some* & *any* und ihre Familien

Wenn du drei CDs kaufen willst, dann sagst du halt „drei".
Und wenn du einige kaufen willst, ohne zu wissen wie
viele? Im Englischen verwendest du dafür **some**. Und wenn
du versehentlich beim Bäcker gelandet bist, der halt keine
CDs hat, dann gibt er dir in England eine Antwort mit **any**.
Wieso? Das erfährst du in diesem Kapitel.

1. Setze *some* oder *any* in den folgenden Sätzen ein –
möglichst richtig.

Tipp

Falls du es nicht mehr genau weißt: Du nimmst *some* bei ganz
normalen Sätzen, aber auch bei höflichen Fragen (mit *please* z.B.).
Sonst nimmst du bei **Fragen** und **Verneinungen** *any*.

a) Let's make _____ fish-burgers. Okay, I'll get _____ fish.

thirsty: durstig

b) I'm thirsty. Can you get me _____ mineral water, please?

c) There aren't _____ bananas. Can you buy _____, please?

d) I wanted to buy _____ cheese, but they didn't have _____.

e) Don't buy _____ more computer games. Save _____ money.

f) Have you got _____ money left?

guys: Typen, Kerle

g) On Thursday Mandy met _____ nice guys at the disco, but today

there aren't _____ interesting people there.

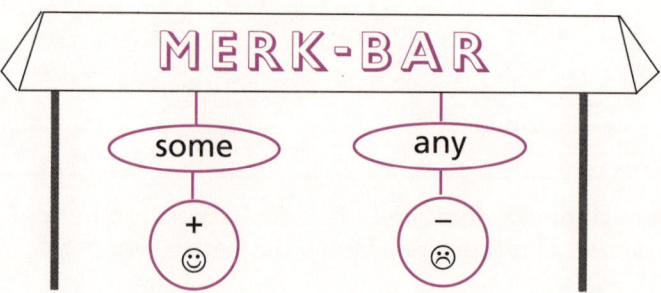

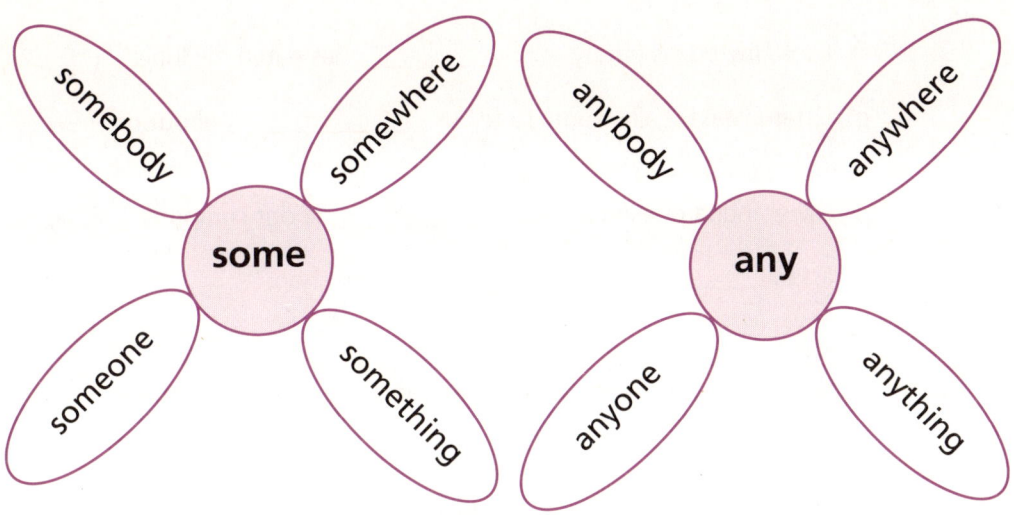

Die Propeller zeigen dir, welche Verbindungen mit *some & any* möglich sind.
Bevor wir mit dem Training beginnen, zuerst ein Blick auf die Beispielsätze.

Aussage	Frage	Verneinung
I want to buy some-thing for my sister's birthday.	Can you think of any-thing?	No, sorry. I can't think of anything.
My new CD must be somewhere.	Is it anywhere in the living room?	No, it isn't. We can't find it anywhere.

birthday: Geburtstag

living room: Wohnzimmer

2. **Setze die passende Form ein.**

a) I'm not thirsty. I don't want _____ to drink.

b) Is there _____ else who wants to tell us some jokes?

c) I left my pen _____ in my friend's bedroom.

d) Hi, John, my scanner isn't working. Can you do _____ ?

e) Where are my new computer games? I can't find them _____.

23

f) Look, my box is empty. _____ has eaten my lunch.

g) Listen please, Sally wants to tell us _____ about her new boyfriend.

h) My grandpa doesn't know _____ about computers. So he

asked _____ in the computer shop.

Q **3.** **Replace the sentences by using *any* and then translate them.**

a) We have no sugar in the house.

We haven't got any sugar in the house.

Wir haben keinen Zucker im Haus. _____.

b) There are no biscuits in my lunch box.

_____

_____

c) My mum has no brothers or sisters.

_____

_____

d) I have no money for this trip.

_____

_____

e) Sorry, I had no time to phone you yesterday.

_____

_____

7   Klein, aber hilfreich: *one* und *ones*

Wieder so eine englische Spezialität, dieses *one*. Aber ganz nützlich, wenn du ein Hauptwort nicht ständig wiederholen willst.

Ohne *one*:

Sally: Give me the glass, please.
Paul: Which glass? The little glass or the big glass?
Sally: The big glass.

Mit *one*:

Sally: Give me the glass, please.
Paul: Which one? The little one or the big one?
Sally: The big one.

Im **Plural (Mehrzahl)** funktioniert es übrigens ganz genauso: mit ***ones***.

1.   Schreibe dieses kleine Gespräch im **Plural (Mehrzahl)** auf.

Der Plural von *glass* ist ***glasses***.   **Tipp**

_____

_____

_____

2.   Ersetze die unterstrichenen Wörter durch *one* oder *ones*.
Übersetze die Sätze anschließend.

a) Which <u>tickets</u> are the cheapest? – The yellow _____ .   *yellow: gelb*

_____

b) Is there <u>a bus stop</u> near here? – Yes, there is _____ over there.

_____

25

c) My cousin knows lots of <u>jokes</u>. I like the _____ about teachers.

_____

d) These <u>cups</u> are dirty. Can we have clean _____, please?

_____

e) My old <u>bike</u> is too small for me now. I think I'll buy a new _____ .

_____

Q **3.** **Use the given parts and make up some more dialogues. Look at the example first.**

bring / teapot   old / new?   new

You: Could you bring me the teapot?
He/she: Which one? The old one or the new one?
You: The new one.

a) show / book   green / yellow?   green

_____

_____

_____

b) Let's count / plates   big / small?   big

_____

_____

_____

c) open / box   on the chair / on the table?   chair

_____

_____

_____

d) I like   that T-shirt over there   long / short?   long

_____

_____

_____

8   Die Artikel: *the, a, an*

Die Artikel „der, die, das" und „ein, eine, ein" sind im Englischen kein Problem. Etwas tückischer ist schon die Frage, wann man den Artikel setzt und wann nicht. Die Beispiele bringen etwas Licht in die Sache, darum fang mit ihnen an, bevor es ans Training geht.

Bestimmter Artikel – *definite article*

She is interested in pop music.	She is interested in **the** pop music of the 90s.
He likes reading books.	He likes reading **the** books his brother gave him.
Life can be wonderful.	**The** lives of children in eastern countries aren't very easy nowadays.
In July school will be over. Great!	This is **the** school my sister went to.

Allgemein gebrauchte Dinge → **ohne Artikel**	Bei bestimmten Dingen → **bestimmter Artikel**

Unbestimmter Artikel – *indefinite article*

She works as **a** bus driver. He is **an** Irishman. It's $6 **a** bottle. We meet twice **a** week.	Bei Berufsbezeichnungen, Nationalitäten, Mengen- und Zeitangaben → **unbestimmter Artikel**

1. *The watchmaker and the timekeeper*
Füge *the, a* oder *an* ein, sodass die Geschichte einen Sinn ergibt.

watchmaker:
Uhrenmacher

There was once _____ old watchmaker who had _____ shop in _____

centre of _____ little town. Every day _____ man stopped by and looked

in _____ window before hurrying on his way.

After _____ year _____ watchmaker one day talked to _____ man and

asked him why he always stopped by _____ window but never entered

_____ shop. _____ man answered, "I'm _____ timekeeper of _____ town,

noon: mittags

and I have to ring _____ church bells at exactly twelve o'clock noon. So

I always check with your clocks in _____ window first."

"Ah", said _____ watchmaker, "but I always set all _____ clocks when I

hear _____ church bells."

Tipp

4-mal *a*, 14-mal *the* und 1-mal *an*.

Q

2. **Put into English.**

a) Sie ist Lehrerin. – b) Die Schule ist aus. – c) Wir sehen ihn dreimal die
Woche. – d) London liegt *(lies)* an *(on)* der Themse *(Thames)*. – e) Magst
du Geschichte *(History)* in der Schule. – f) Sie kommen aus den
Niederlanden *(Netherlands)*. – g) Zu viel Zucker ist nicht gut für dich. –
h) Was für eine interessante Geschichte *(story)*!

_____

_____

_____

_____

_____

_____

9 Pronomen mit *-self / -selves*

I can do it **myself**.	Ich kann es selbst tun.
You can do it **yourself**.	Du kannst es selbst tun.
She can do it **herself**.	Sie kann es selbst tun.
He can do it **himself**.	Er kann es selbst tun.
It can do it **itself**.	Es kann es selbst tun.
We can do it **ourselves**.	Wir können es selbst tun.
You can do it **yourselves**.	Ihr könnt es selbst tun.
They can do it **themselves**.	Sie können es selbst tun.

Wenn das klar ist, dann wird die nächste Übung keinen Stress bereiten.

1. **Setze die richtigen Reflexivpronomen ein. Schau auf die Beispielsätze.**

a) I've just bought _____ a new pair of shoes.

b) I don't like people who always talk about _____.

c) Our parrot looked at _____ in the mirror and went silent.

d) Hey, you two. Enjoy your trip and look after _____.

e) We had a great time in Berlin. We really enjoyed _____.

f) Don't be shy, Sally, help _____ to the biscuits.

g) My brother failed the driving test and now he's angry with _____.

h) Jenny was careless with the new knife and cut _____.

2. **Unterschiede zwischen dem Deutschen und Englischen. Übersetze.**

Achtung! Nur zwei dieser Sätze benötigen im Englischen ein Reflexivpronomen.

Tipp

a) Ich kann mich nicht erinnern, wo sie wohnt.

   I can't remember where she lives. _____

b) Wenn du dein Fahrrad nicht selbst reparieren kannst, kann ich dir helfen.

_____

c) Schließ die Tür hinter dir zu.

_____

d) Es ereignete *(happen)* sich am Freitag.

_____

e) Manche Leute *(people)* sprechen mit sich selbst.

_____

f) Die Frauen trafen *(meet, met, met)* sich vor dem Café.

_____

g) Sally hat sich sehr verändert *(has changed)* seit dem letzten Jahr.

_____

Doctor, doctor, I keep talking to myself. What can I do? –
Just walk around with a mobile phone.

10 Possessivpronomen klären Eigentumsverhältnisse

This is **my** bike. It's **mine**.
That is **your** skateboard. It's **yours**.
Is it **his** pen? Yes, it's **his**.
Here's **her** magazine. It's **hers**.
That is **our** gym. It's **ours**.
There are **your** rooms. They're **yours**.
Are these **their** shoes?
Yes, they are **theirs**.

Das ist mein Fahrrad. Es ist meins.
Das ist dein Skateboard. Es ist deins.
Ist es sein Stift? Ja, es ist seiner.
Hier ist ihre Zeitschrift. Es ist ihre.
Das ist unsere Sporthalle. Es ist unsere.
Dort sind eure Zimmer. Sie sind eure.
Sind das ihre Schuhe?
Ja, es sind ihre.

Schau dir die Beispiele noch einmal genau an, denn gleich geht's an die Übungen.

1. Setze die passende Form ein.

a) Does this book belong to your father? – Yes, it's _____.

belong to: gehören

b) But all the other books belong to my grandparents. They are _____.

c) Whose are these shirts? Are they all _____, Jill? – Yes, they are _____.

d) Hey, you two, are these your biros? – Yes, they are _____.

biro: Kugelschreiber

e) This can't be your T-shirt. _____ is longer. It must be my T-shirt.

_____ is short.

f) These magazines belong to Christine. They are _____.

g) This photo here is nice. Is it yours, Phil? – No, it's not _____.

It belongs to my brother. It's _____.

2. Setze das richtige Wort in die Lücken ein. Die Beispiele oben können dir dabei helfen.

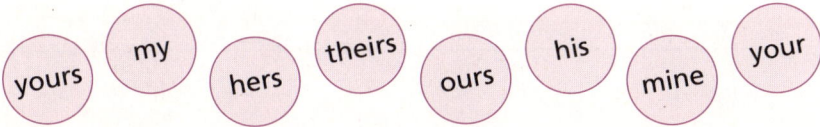

yours   my   hers   theirs   ours   his   mine   your

a) I can't find _____ biro. – Oh, there's one in the kitchen.

Perhaps it's _____.

b) Is this computer _____, Cindy? – No, it's not _____. It belongs

to _____ brother. _____ is in the computer shop for repairs.

So _____ brother gave me _____ for _____ homework.

c) Whose is that old car in _____ garage, Brenda? It isn't _____,

is it? – No, it belongs to _____ grandparents. Dad has given them

_____ for a short trip. There's something wrong with _____. Dad

wanted to have a look at it.

d) Where is _____ bike, Ronny? – Well, _____ sister is away with it.

_____ has broken down again.

Tipp

Erinnerst du dich? Wenn du *my, your, her* usw. verwendest, dann brauchst du immer noch ein Hauptwort (Nomen, Substantiv) dabei. Anders ist es bei *mine, yours, hers* usw. Die können ohne ein Hauptwort stehen.

3. Übersetze b) und d) aus Übung 2 ins Deutsche.

b) _____

_____

_____

d) _____

_____

_____

11 Leicht zu verwechselnde Wörter

> Wenn du im Wörterbuch ein Wort nachschaust, dann findest du manchmal zwei oder mehr englische Entsprechungen. Welches englische Wort ist aber das richtige für das, was du sagen willst? Hier kannst du besonders häufige dieser *tricky pairs* trainieren, was dir so manche Peinlichkeit erspart.

1. Die englische Entsprechung für „bringen"

bring ⟵ (**bringen**) ⟶ take

Could you **bring** me a glass, please?	I'll **take** this glass to the kitchen.
Könntest du mir ein Glas bringen? = **her**bringen	Ich bringe das Glas in die Küche. = **hin**bringen

Übersetze.

a) Wer kann Tante Anne zum Bahnhof bringen?

_____

b) Bringt morgen bitte eure Notizen *(notes)* mit.

_____

c) Meine Schwester hat ihren neuen Freund mit nach Hause gebracht.

_____

d) Kannst du diesen Eimer *(bucket)* zu unserem Nachbarn bringen?

_____

Überlege immer, ob etwas oder jemand **her**gebracht oder **hin**gebracht wird.

Tipp

2. Die englische Entsprechung für „tragen"

wear ◄──────── (tragen) ─────────► carry

She is **wearing** her
new T-shirt.

Sie hat ihr neues
T-Shirt an.

= etwas anhaben

Übersetze.

a) Er trägt seine neuen Jeans. _____

b) Er trägt eine Kiste mit Jeans. _____

c) Ich sollte einen Pullover tragen. _____

d) Müssen wir unser Gepäck selbst tragen?

Do we have to _____

Let me **carry** this
heavy bag for you.

Lass mich diese
schwere Tasche
tragen.

= schleppen

3. Die englische Entsprechung für „zwischen"

between ◄──────── (zwischen) ─────────► among

Michael is standing **between**
Jill and Janet.

Michael steht zwischen Jill
und Janet.

= zwischen **zwei** Personen, Dingen
Ereignissen

He feels fine **among**
pretty girls.

Er fühlt sich gut
zwischen / unter
hübschen Mädchen.
= zwischen **mehr als**
zwei

Übersetze.

a) Ihr Geburtstag ist zwischen Weihnachten und Silvester *(New Year's Eve)*.

Her birthday is _____

b) Möchtest du zwischen Harry und Oliver sitzen?

Would you like to sit _____

c) Ich wartete zwischen all den Kisten.

I was waiting _____

d) Das Buch war zwischen den Zeitungen *(newspapers)*.

_____

Weißt du noch: zwischen **zwei** Dingen oder Personen: ***between***, sonst ***among***.

Tipp

4. **Die englische Entsprechung für „machen"**

make ⟵—————— (machen) ——————⟶ do

Jason **makes** breakfast
on Sundays.

My sister **does** the
washing up and I **do**
the cleaning.

Jason macht sonntags
das Frühstück.

My Schwester macht
den Abwasch und ich
mache sauber.

= etwas **herstellen**

= etwas **erledigen**

Übersetze:

a) Hast du deine Hausaufgaben gemacht?

_____

b) Wir müssen Pläne machen. _____

c) Sie hat einen neuen Anfang *(start)* gemacht.

_____

d) Wer macht heute sauber? _____

5. Die englische Entsprechung für „wenn, falls"

if ◄────── (falls/wenn) ──────► when

If I go shopping, | When I go shopping
I'll buy you that CD. | I'll buy you that CD.

If I go shopping,
I'll buy you that CD.

Falls ich einkaufen
gehe, kaufe ich dir
diese CD.

= **falls** = ich bin mir **nicht**
sicher, dass ich es tun werde

When I go shopping
I'll buy you that CD.

Wenn ich einkaufen
gehe, kaufe ich dir
diese CD.

= **wenn** = ich bin mir
sicher, dass ich es tue

Übersetze:

a) Falls Oma anruft, sag ihr, wir sind okay.

_____

b) Wenn wir am Bahnhof sind, müssen wir an die Fahrkarten denken.

_____

c) Ich werde zu Hause sein, wenn du kommst.

_____

d) Wenn du willst, werde ich deinem Lehrer ein Fax schicken.

_____

**Falls du im Deutschen „wenn" durch „falls" ersetzen kannst, dann
ist im Englischen immer *if* richtig.**

If / When werden auch gern für Graffiti gebraucht:

When I'm right, nobody remembers. When I'm wrong, nobody forgets!

bloody silly:
saublöde

If R.E.P. is the answer, it must be a bloody silly question.

6. Die englische Entsprechung für „welcher, welche, welches"

what ←——— (welcher, welche, welches) ———→ which

What's your telephone number?

Which of these numbers is for your mobile phone?

Welche Telefonnummer hast du?

Welche dieser Nummern ist für dein Handy?

= Auswahl unbestimmt

= bestimmte Auswahl

Übersetze.

a) Welche Sprache *(language)* spricht dieser Mann?

_____

b) Welche der europäischen Sprachen findest *(think)* du leicht?

_____

c) Welches ist dein Lieblingssport *(favourite sport)*?

_____

d) Welche T-Shirts magst du lieber, die grünen oder die gelben?

_____

12 Unterschiede zwischen dem britischen und amerikanischen Englisch

Wenn du „Zippverschluss" hörst, dann weißt du vielleicht nicht, wovon die Rede ist, weil du dafür das Wort „Reißverschluss" verwendest. Ähnlich ist es mit dem British English (kürzen wir BE ab) und dem American English (AE). Da gibt es teils unterschiedliche Wörter, manchmal ist auch nur die Schreibung anders.

Schauen wir uns zuerst einige **unterschiedliche Wörter** an:

GB	D	USA
shop	Laden	store
sweets	Süßigkeiten	candy / candies
biscuits	Kekse	cookies
lorry	Lastwagen	truck
petrol	Benzin	gas
motorway	Autobahn	freeway
autumn	Herbst	fall
Underground	U-Bahn	subway
head teacher	Schulleiter(in)	principal
lift	Fahrstuhl	elevator
flat	Wohnung	apartment
cinema	Kino	movie
phone box	Telefonzelle	phone booth
city centre	Innenstadt	downtown
pupil	Schüler(in)	student

Bei einigen Wörtern ist nur die **Schreibung unterschiedlich**, zum Beispiel:

programme	Programm	program
dialogue	Dialog	dialog
tyre	Reifen	tire
centre	Zentrum	center
theatre	Theater	theater
colour	Farbe	color
neighbour	Nachbar	neighbor
travelling	Reise(n)	traveling

Bestimmt ist es dir aufgefallen, dass im AE die Wörter meist mit weniger Buchstaben auskommen.

 **Tipp**

1. Ordne richtig zu.

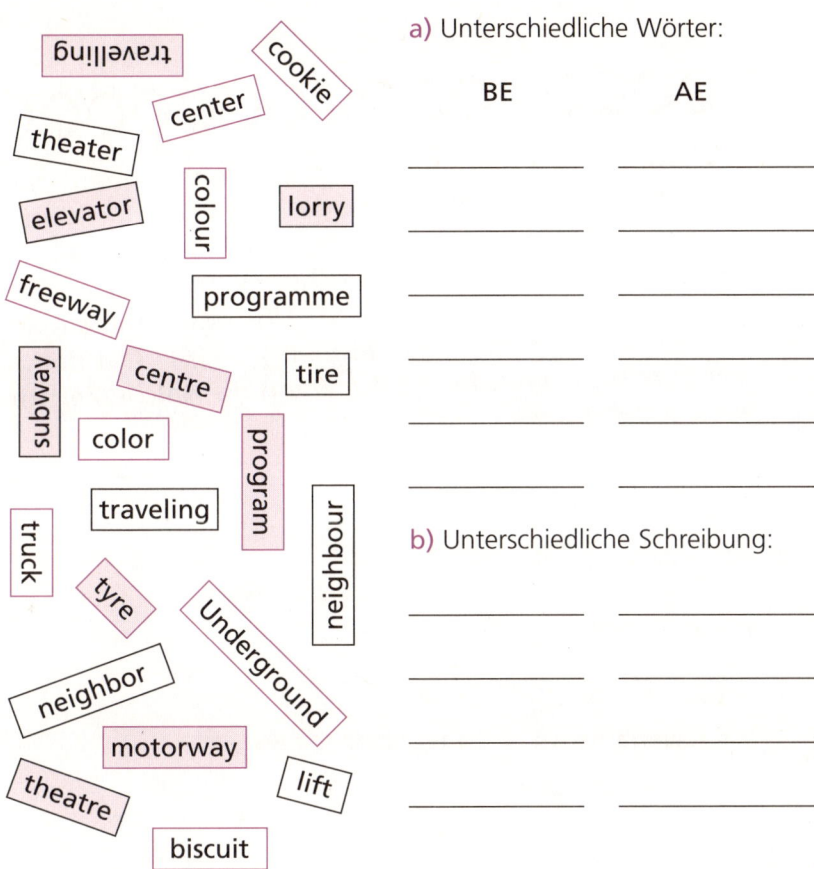

a) Unterschiedliche Wörter:

     BE   AE

_____   _____

_____   _____

_____   _____

_____   _____

_____   _____

_____   _____

b) Unterschiedliche Schreibung:

_____   _____

_____   _____

_____   _____

_____   _____

2. Schreibe diesen Text so um, dass aus den amerikanischen Millers brititsche Millers werden. Beachte dabei die unterstrichenen Wörter.

The Millers live in a nice <u>apartment</u>. Mr Miller is a <u>principal</u>. And Mrs. Miller works in a <u>store</u>. Their two children go to school and are good <u>students</u>. Once a month all the Millers take the <u>subway</u> and go to the <u>movies</u>. There they eat lots of <u>cookies</u> and <u>candies</u>.

apartment: Wohnung
principal: Schulleiter

The Millers live in a nice flat. ...

Schreib den Text in dein Heft ab und markiere die geänderten Wörter.

 **Tipp**

B Workshop Grammar

1 Die Vergangenheitsformen

Willkommen zu einer Reise in die Vergangenheit! Mit diesem Kapitel verschaffst du dir einen Überblick über die verschiedenen Möglichkeiten im Englischen, über vergangene Ereignisse zu sprechen. Wann verwendet man die einfache Form (1, 3, 5)? Und wann muss man die Verlaufsform mit -ing nehmen (2, 4, 6)? Auf den folgenden Seiten erfährst du, wann du welche Zeitform verwenden musst.

Zeitformen im Überblick

① **present perfect**

1. She **has bought** these shoes.
2. We **haven't heard** of the results of the tests yet.
3. They**'ve** already **taken** their seats.

---

1. Wenn eine Handlung bereits geschehen ist, der **Zeitpunkt** aber **nicht so wichtig** ist, benutzt du das *present perfect*. Im Mittelpunkt stehen die **Ergebnisse** der Handlung.
2. Das *present perfect* verwendest du auch, wenn du über Handlungen sprichst, deren **Ergebnisse noch nicht bekannt** sind, und die noch andauern.
3. Und schließlich brauchst du das *present perfect*, wenn die Ergebnisse einer zurückliegenden Handlung in der **Gegenwart** sichtbar sind.

② present perfect progressive

He **has been working** with his new software since lunch.

> Wenn die **Dauer einer Handlung** wichtig ist und die Handlung noch
> weitergeht, verwendest du das *present perfect progressive*.

③ simple past

1. We **went** to the cinema last night.

2. We **stopped** and **talked** to the old man at the entrance.
   He **told** us about his problems.

> 1. Du nimmst *simple past,* wenn im Satz Formulierungen wie *last
>   night, last month, yesterday* oder *three hours ago* vorkommen.
> 2. Das *simple past* verwendest du auch, um über Dinge zu erzählen, die
>   sich in der Vergangenheit abgespielt haben. Wenn sich ein Ereignis
>   nach dem anderen abgespielt hat, dann nimmst du für jedes Ereignis
>   *simple past (we stopped ... and talked ... he told ...).*

④ past progressive

I **was playing** my new computer game
when suddenly the lights **went** out.

> Wenn du ausdrücken möchtest, was du zu einem bestimmten Zeitpunkt
> in der Vergangenheit gerade gemacht hast, dann musst du das *past
> progressive* nehmen. Als die Lichter ausgingen, hast du gerade das
> neue Computer Spiel gespielt *(was playing my new ...).*

⑤ past perfect

When we **reached** the bus, the storm **had** already **started**.

> Wenn du über zwei Ereignisse berichtest, die sich in der Vergangenheit
> abspielten, dann nimmst du *past perfect* für das **frühere** und *simple
> past* für das **spätere**. In unserem Beispiel hat zuerst der Sturm losgelegt
> *(had started)* und dann erreichten wir den Bus *(reached)*. Berichtest du
> über ein Ereignis nach dem anderen, dann nimmst du wieder *simple
> past* (➜ ③).

⑥ **past perfect progressive**

I **had been waiting** in front of the cinema for 20 minutes
when the rain **stopped**.

Hier funktioniert alles genauso wie beim *past perfect* bis auf einen
Unterschied: Die *progressive*-Form brauchst du, wenn du den Zeitraum
betonen willst. Wenn es dich ziemlich genervt hat, zwanzig Minuten vor
dem Kino zu warten, dann nimmst du besser *I had been waiting for 20
minutes ....*

---

since und *for*

Wenn du angeben möchtest, seit wann du schon wartest, dann brauchst
du *since* (seit) dafür. Angenommen du möchtest sagen, dass du seit halb
acht gewartet hast, als der Regen endlich aufhörte:

I had been waiting in front of the cinema **since** half past seven (7.30)
when the rain stopped.

Im Beispiel oben (→ ⑥) drückst du den **Zeitraum** *(for 20 minutes)* mit
for aus und in diesem Beispiel hier den **Zeitpunkt** *(since half past seven)*
mit *since*. Das gilt natürlich auch für *present perfect* und *present
perfect progressive*.

MERK-BAR

since mit dem '**i**' ...

'**i**' mit dem Punkt ...

since für den ZEITPUNKT !

1. Verbformen
Waagrecht findest du 12 unregelmäßige Verben, und zwar deren
zweite Form. Und **Senkrecht** sind es ebenfalls 12 Verben, doch dies-
mal deren **dritte Form**. Schreibe sie in die jeweiligen Spalten.

V	W	X	Y	C	Z	S	S	A	N	G	G	F	E	D	F	O	R	G	O	T	C	B	A	W
U	B	T	T	H	R	E	W	S	D	R	Q	E	P	O	M	K	J	S	H	O	W	E	D	R
T	E	J	H	O	G	E	U	F	R	E	S	A	W	D	C	B	A	P	I	N	L	J	H	I
S	C	Z	Y	S	X	N	M	H	I	D	W	T	V	U	G	T	S	O	D	R	Z	F	W	T
T	O	O	K	E	Q	P	D	O	V	N	M	E	L	K	I	J	J	K	D	H	Y	L	V	T
R	M	R	A	N	W	R	O	T	E	G	F	N	E	D	V	C	B	E	E	A	X	O	U	E
Q	E	M	L	K	J	J	N	H	N	G	F	E	F	L	E	W	D	N	N	C	B	W	A	N
P	O	N	M	C	A	M	E	L	K	J	J	H	G	F	N	E	D	C	B	R	A	N	G	A

run – _____ – run

ring – _____ – rung

see – _____ – seen

show – _____ – shown

sing – _____ – sung

write – _____ – written

throw – _____ – thrown

take – _____ – taken

hide – _____ – hidden

forget – _____ – forgotten

fly – _____ – flown

come – _____ – come

become – became – _____

choose – chose – _____

do – did – _____

drive – drove – _____

eat – ate – _____

fly – flew – _____

give – gave – _____

hide – hid – _____

speak – spoke – _____

see – saw – _____

swim – swam – _____

write – wrote – _____

2.　Fragen

Du weißt nicht, ob es schon geschehen ist. Also bildest du Fragen und verwendest dabei das *present perfect*.

a) Susan/Kevin – do their homework.

　　Have Susan and Kevin done their homework?

b) Janet – make her bed.

　　_____

c) Richard – take the dogs for a walk.

　　_____

d) Your grandparents – buy a new computer.

　　_____

e) dad – forget his password.

　　_____

f) Your sister – buy a new computer game.

　　_____

Tipp　Weißt du noch? Bei *he, she it* nimmst du *has*.

MERK-BAR

buy – bought – bought is like bring – brought – brought

take – took – taken is like shake – shook – shaken

sleep – slept – slept is like keep – kept – kept …

Kannst du weitere Reime bilden?

3. *Little Red Riding Hood today*
Bevor sich Rotkäppchen auf den Weg zur Großmutter macht,
muss sie sich viele Fragen von der Mutter anhören.
Übertrage sie ins Englische und verwende *present perfect*.

a) Hast du Großmutters E-Mail gelesen? **(read)**

   Have you read grandma's email?

b) Hast du deiner Lehrerin schon die Hausarbeiten gefaxt? **(fax)**

   _____

c) Hast du die Checkliste für den Korb geschrieben? **(write)**

   _____

d) Hast du den Film über die Killerwölfe gesehen? **(see)**

   _____

e) Hast du den Wetterbericht gehört? **(hear / weather forecast)**

   _____

f) Hast du Großmutters neues Computerspiel in den Korb getan? **(put)**

   _____

4. Vervollständige die Sätze. Nimm eins der vorgegebenen Verben.
Entscheide, ob du *simple past* oder *present perfect* nehmen musst.

a) I *have_____* *bought_____* a new CD.

   Do you want to listen to it?

b) Oh dear! It's beginning to rain and

   I _____ _____my raincoat.

c) Oh, hello David! Where _____ you _____ ?

   I _____ _____ _____ you for weeks!

d) Sorry I'm late. _____ the play _____ yet?

e) Yes, sorry. The performance _____ 30 minutes ago.

f) Grandpa _____ for a short visit last week.

buy

forget

have

be

not see

begin

start

come

Q

5. Have you ever? … – When did you? …
Ask questions using *present perfect* or *simple past*. Give answers to
these questions. Follow the example given.

a) (see a horror film) _Have you ever seen a horror film_ ? – _Yes, I have._

   (last week) _When did you see it_ ? – _I saw it last week._

b) (have a virus in software) _____

   _____ ? – _____

   (three months ago) _____? – _____

c) (eat a vegetable kebab) _____? –

   _____

   (last Saturday) _____? – _____

d) (sing a French song) _____ ? –

   _____

   (three weeks ago) _____? – _____

e) (visit Switzerland) _____ ? –

   _____

   (last year) _____? – _____

Q

6. What were people doing when …?
Put the verbs in brackets into the right tense. Choose between
simple past and *past progressive*.

a) Kevin _was reading_ (**read**) a comic when he _heard_

   (**hear**) a noise downstairs.

b) The children _____(**play**) in the playground when

   the rain _____ (**start**).

c) When Jenny _____ (come) home, her grandfather

_____ (repair) his bike.

d) Simon _____ (not watch) TV when Ronny

_____ (phone). He _____ (do)

his homework.

e) My grandparents _____ (leave) the house when

a police car _____ (stop) in front of them.

f) When my sister and I _____ (paint) the

garage door, our uncle _____ (arrive).

7. Fragen, Fragen!
Bilde Fragen und verwende dabei *present perfect*.

a) (Ronny/Simon) – do their homework)
   Have Ronny and Simon done their homework?

b) (Kate – give the cat some milk)

_____

c) (Robert – find his new CDs)

_____

d) (grandma and grandpa – come home)

_____

e) (dad – take the dogs for a walk)

_____

f) (you – buy the cinema tickets)

_____

g) (the dog – get its food)

_____

8. Neinsager gesucht:
Verneine die folgenden Aussagesätze.

a) The train came in early. –   *The train didn't come in early.*

b) My friends have gone shopping. –_____

_____

c) My grandpa has written me an e-mail. – _____

_____

d) My brother took the bus. –_____

e) Our teacher has bought this CD. – _____

_____

f) I did the washing-up. – _____

g) I could hear you. – _____

Achtung: Im *present perfect* und übrigens auch im *past perfect*
verneinst du Sätze **ohne** eine Form von **do**. Also: *I haven't gone
shopping.*

9. *Scrambled sentences* – Bilde richtige Sätze.

a) has / David / never / My / eaten / food. / Chinese / friend /

My friend David has never eaten Chinese food.

b) mother / Has / heard / your / good / news? / the /

_____

c) all / kitchen. / Our / finished / the / hasn't / in / dad / yet. / jobs / the /

_____

_____

d) yesterday. / a / visit / My / for / aunt / came

_____

e) to / gone / Ireland / a / for / Our / holiday. / neighbours / have

_____

_____

f) Poor Mrs Robins! dog / Her / week. / old / last / died

_____

10. Redeabsichten
Du willst sagen, erzählen, mitteilen, dass …

a) … man deinen Großvater ins Krankenhaus gebracht hat.

They have taken my grandpa to hospital.

b) … er schon sechs Wochen lang krank war.

_____

c) … alles vor sieben Wochen mit einer schlimmen (bad) Erkältung (cold) begann.

_____

d) … der Arzt am Anfang nicht wusste, welche Medizin die beste sein würde.

_____

_____

e) … dein Großvater nun schon seit Dienstag im Krankenhaus ist.

_____

_____

Q

11. You can't please everyone.
Put in the correct form of the verb – *past tense* or *past perfect*?

*to please every-
one: es jedem
recht machen*

decide	One day a farmer and his son _____ to sell their horse at a village market, seven miles away from their home. After they
leave; call	had _____ the farm, a neighbour _____ to them: "Why are you both walking when you have a horse?" After
hear, ride	they _____ _____ this the son _____ and
walk; go	the farmer _____ by his side. After they _____
come	_____ on for two miles, two women _____
say	along and one of them _____:
	"Look at that boy. He's younger than his father, but the old man
ride; walk	has to walk." Then the father _____ and the son _____.
go	After they _____ _____ nearly halfway, two men
come; say	_____ along and _____: "Why must that poor
	man walk? Isn't your horse strong enough to carry you both?"
climb	So the boy _____ onto the horse too, and they both
ride	_____ on. They had been riding on for a while
shout	when some children _____ : "Look at that poor
	horse. It has to carry two big men. Why don't you carry your
be	horse for a change? And that _____ exactly what they
do, tie	_____ in the end. After they _____
put	_____ the horse to a pole which they _____
carry	over their shoulders, they _____ it straight into the village.
never see	The people at the market _____ anything like it
laugh	before. They _____ about "the farmer and his son
try	who _____ to please everyone."

12. The "thing"

The following text is about a strange encounter. Some verbs suffered hard from it, mainly their vowels (a, e, i, o, u). Put it right again by completing the verbs.

encounter: Begegnung

Some boys were _____ in a barn near a field in Portugal.
(wrkng)

barn: Scheune

They _____ a dog with them, and this dog suddenly
(hd)

_____ barking outside. When one of the boys
(strtd)

_____ outside to look, he _____ a strange
(wnt)   (sw)

"thing" with a big head and a small body. It _____ like a man
(lkd)

but it _____ a man. It was _____ in the
(wsn't)   (stndng)

middle of the field. The boy _____ afraid and _____
(ws)   (bgn)

to throw stones at it. But this "thing" _____ react. The boy
(ddn't)

_____ to touch it, but something hit him hard. He
(wnt)

_____ see what it _____, but it hurt him like hell.
(cldn't)   (ws)

hurt like hell: tat höllisch weh

He _____ back into the barn, the dog after him. And from there they
(rn)

all _____ the "thing" move away in a cloud of blue light. The
(wtchd)

next day the police _____ a photo of a large patch of burnt
(tk)

patch: Fleck

grass in the middle of the field.

2   Einfache Formen und Verlaufsformen

Es ist nicht einfach, im Englischen die richtige Zeitform zu wählen. Besonders knifflig ist es mit den Verlaufsformen oder -ing-Formen. Schau die Übersicht an, dann wird dir bestimmt vieles klarer. Und anschließend wird eine Runde trainiert, damit es auch im Test klappt.

SIMPLE FORM

	Mitteilungsabsicht	Beispiel
present tense	Man tut es oft oder regelmäßig (oder auch selten, nie, gelegentlich usw.) Es werden aufeinander folgende Handlungen beschrieben. Es geht um organisierte, zeitlich geregelte Abläufe. Es werden Tatsachen geäußert.	We **often** **go** to the cinema. They **never** **complain**. First we **go** to the station. There we **buy** our tickets. Then we **take** the train downtown. After that… Assembly **begins** at nine o'clock. Lunch break **ends** at half past one. Hull **lies** on Humber. The river Humber **flows** into the North Sea.
present perfect	Es ist irgendwann, ganz gleich wann, etwas gemacht worden. Das Ergebnis ist sichtbar. Eine Zeitangabe, wie *last week, yesterday, last summer*, kommt im Satz nicht vor.	She **has taken** this wonderful photo. **Have** you **heard** about that new film? *Hast du von diesem neuen Film gehört?* What **has he told** them?
past tense	Wenn du eine Zeitangabe, wie *last week, last year, yesterday, two weeks ago* usw. im Satz hast, dann liegst du mit *past tense* richtig.	My sister **went** to Boston **last year**. **Did** you **enjoy** the concert **last night**?
past perfect	Berichtest du von zwei Ereignissen in der Vergangenheit, dann nimmst du für das weiter zurückliegende *past perfect*: Erst war das Konzert zu Ende, dann nahmen sie einen Imbiss.	When we **arrived** at the snack bar, we **found** Sue and Terry there already. Their concert **had finished** early.

PROGRESSIVE FORM

	Mitteilungsabsicht	Beispiel
present tense	Du berichtest über etwas, das gerade geschieht.	The sun is shining. *Die Sonne scheint gerade.*
	Es werden Trends und Entwicklungen beschrieben.	Prices are going up all the time. *Die Preise steigen ständig.*
	Es sollen Emotionen wie z. B. Ärger, Zweifel oder Überraschung ausgedrückt werden. (Adverbien wie *always, forever, constantly* usw. deuten das an.)	He is always bullying my sister. Are you telling me that this is true?
present perfect	Eine Handlung hat bis jetzt angedauert, sie wird aber wohl noch weitergehen. Meist kommen Wörter wie *since* oder *for* darin vor.	My sister has been waiting for the bus since two o'clock now. *Meine Schwester wartet schon seit zwei Uhr auf den Bus.* We have been visiting the chatroom for 30 minutes. *Wir sind schon seit 30 Minuten …*
past tense	Es geht um zwei Handlungen in der Vergangenheit: Eine fand gerade statt *(were playing)*, als eine andere hinzukam *(the thunderstorm began)*.	We were playing football when the thunderstorm began. *Wir spielten gerade Fußball als das Gewitter begann.* My sister was washing her hair when the lights went out. *Meine Schwester hat sich gerade die Haare gewaschen, als die Lichter ausgingen.*
past perfect	Alles wie beim *past perfect simple*, nur dass du mit dem *progressive* wieder die Handlung betonst.	We had been waiting for our plane for two hours when the news about the pilots' strike came in. *Wir **hatten schon** zwei Stunden auf das Flugzeug **gewartet**, als die Nachricht vom Pilotenstreik **hereinkam**.*

1. YES or NO?
Schreibe das Gegenteil zu der jeweiligen Aussage hin.

a) They don't often visit museums. – _They often visit museums._

b) It's raining. – _____

c) He has been waiting for us. – _____

d) I wasn't sleeping when you phoned me. – _____

e) They won't arrive before nine o'clock. – _____

f) She is always asking silly questions. – _____

2. Oh, these i-devils!
Ganz teuflisch! Jetzt haben die *i-devils* zugeschlagen und in den
folgenden Sätzen jedes einzelne **i** verschwinden lassen. Kannst du
das wieder in Ordnung bringen?

a) My sster enjoyed the new flm. – _My sister enjoyed the new film._

b) The sun was shnng when we vsted our grandmother. –_____

_____

c) What were you dong when the lghts went out? – _____

_____

d) Dd you gve hm hs comcs? – _____

e) t wll ran a bt n the evenng. – _____

f) He wll be sttng at hs computer when we arrve. – _____

_____

g) We have been watng snce sx o'clock. – _____

_____

3. Translation.
Write the following sentences in English.

_Q_

a) Bist du schon einmal in einem Fitnessstudio gewesen? – _Have you_

ever been to a fitness studio?

b) Ja, ich gehe regelmäßig dort hin. – _____

_____

_regelmäßig:
regularly_

c) Letzte Woche bin ich nicht hingegangen. – _____

_____

d) Meine Schwester war krank. – _____

e) Ich musste mich um sie kümmern. _____

_kümmern um:
care for_

f) Ich kümmere mich immer um sie, wenn sie krank ist. – _____

_____

4. Questions, questions…
Write the correct short answers. (+) = yes; (–) = no

a) Has the train arrived yet? (–) _No, it hasn't._

b) Have your friends been to the computer shop? (+) _____

c) Have you bought this new CD? (–) _____

d) Do your grandparents speak French? (+) _____

e) Are you tired? (–) _____

f) Did you phone your brother yesterday? (+) _____

Q

5. Rip van Winkle
Übertrage den folgenden Text ins Englische. Achte dabei auf die
Verben und Zeitformen.

Amerikanische Kinder kennen die Geschichte von Rip van Winkle.
Dieser Mann lebte in Amerika vor 200 Jahren. Er liebte das
Leben, ging gern in die Kneipe und traf sich mit Freunden. Seine
Frau mochte das nicht. Eines schönen Morgens, als seine Frau
zum Markt gegangen war, rief er seinen Hund, nahm sein
Gewehr und ging zum Jagen in die Berge. Aber dort fühlte er
sich müde und legte sich schlafen. Als er aufwachte, sah alles um
ihn herum ganz anders aus. Viele Dinge hatten sich verändert.
Das Dorf war größer geworden. Die Leute kannten ihn nicht. Sie
trugen auch andere Kleidung. Und wo sein Hund hingegangen
war, konnte ihm keiner sagen. Sein Haus war sehr alt geworden
und niemand wohnte mehr darin. Und so wurde es ihm langsam
klar, dass er viele Jahre geschlafen hatte.

American children know the story of Rip van Winkle. This man

_____

_____

_____

_____

_____

_____

_____

_____

_____

_____

_____

6. Time for some jokes

Wenn du richtig ergänzt, dann bekommst du einige „gespenstische" Witze.

a) Where do snowmen go to dance? –

_____

The Vampire State Building

Have you eaten anyone already?

b) What do sea monsters eat? –

_____

With a witch watch.

Oh, it's you!

c) How does a witch tell the time? –

_____

witch: Hexe

He had no body to dance with.

d) What did the cannibal say when he was late for dinner? –

_____

Fish and ships.

skeleton: Skelett

e) Why didn't the skeleton enjoy the party?

_____

To a snowball

To get to the second-hand shop.

f) Why did the man with one hand cross the street? –

_____

famous: berühmt

g) What famous building did Dracula visit when he went to New York? –

_____

stupid: blöde

h) Have you heard about the stupid person who goes around saying 'NO'? –

No! _____

3 Zukunft

Wenn du im Englischen über zukünftige Ereignisse sprechen möchtest, dann hast du verschiedene Formen zur Auswahl, je nachdem, was du genau sagen willst. Wann nimmst du aber welche Form? Hier erfährst du es genau.

	Das willst du sagen	Diese Form brauchst du	Beispiele
①	a) Du hast etwas fest vor.	going to + Infinitiv	I'm going to write all the events down in my diary.
	b) Du siehst eindeutige Anzeichen dafür, dass etwas geschieht.		Look at those waves! We're going to have a rough passage. *Schau dir diese Wellen an, wir werden ein raue Überfahrt haben.*
②	a) Du drückst deine Hoffnung aus.		I hope the passage won't be too rough. *Ich hoffe, die Überfahrt wird nicht zu rau werden.*
	c) Du drückst eine Vermutung aus.	will / won't (= will not)	The performance will probably last a bit longer today. *Die Vorstellung wird wohl etwas länger dauern.*
	d) Du hast dich spontan für etwas entschieden.		That bag is too heavy for you. I will / I'll help you. *Diese Tasche ist zu schwer für dich. Ich helfe dir.*
③	Du hast etwas fest vor und kannst auch schon sagen, wann es geschehen wird.	verb + ing (present progressive)	I am flying to Florida next week. *Nächste Woche werde ich nach Florida fliegen.*

1. Fragen mit *going to*

Person A: what / you / do? *What are you going to do?* _____

Person B: Write an e-mail. *I'm going to write an e-mail.* _____

A: Who / you / write to? *Who are you going to write to?* _____

B: Uncle Henry. _____

A: you / buy / a new computer game? _____
B: Yes, I am.
A: What kind / you / get? _____
B: A game with aliens, I think.

A: where / spend / your next holiday? _____

aliens: Außer-irdische, Fremde

_____
B: In Florida.
A: you / visit / Kennedy Space Center? _____
B: Yes, I am / Yes, we are.

A: what / you / do / on Friday afternoon? _____

_____
B: I'm going to the fitness centre.
A: how long / you / stay there? _____
B: About three hours.

A: how / you / get / to Dublin? _____
B: By plane.
A: when / you / leave? _____
B: Next Saturday.

A: what / you / buy / for your cousin's birthday? _____

_____
B: I don't know.
A: she / have / a birthday party? _____
B: Yes.

A: you / paint / your room? _____
B: Yes.
A: what colour / you / do it? _____
B: Yellow.

paint: malen, anstreichen

Q **2.** What are they going to do?
Schreibe auf, was sie vorhaben.

a) Linda holt ihren Fotoapparat heraus: *She is going to take*

some photos.

b) Jim kommt mit seinem Fußball aus dem Haus. _____

_____

c) Ben packt seine Gitarre aus. _____

d) Becky stopft ihre Jeans in die Waschmaschine. _____

_____

e) Jenny öffnet eine Dose Katzenfutter. _____

f) Harry kommt mit Zutaten für eine Pizza vom Einkauf. _____

_____

g) Mutter schreibt einen Einkaufszettel. _____

h) Tessa blättert im Telefonbuch. _____

i) Der Arzt setzt sich an Kims Bett. _____

j) Vater holt das Fahrrad aus der Garage. _____

_____

MERK-BAR

Where are you going to go today?

In vielen Fällen kann man's gleich sehen:

Dieses und jenes wird bestimmt geschehen.

going to – ist doch klar!

3. The going-to-go-stories
Suche dir einige Buchstaben aus dem Alphabet und schreibe
schräge Geschichten oder Dialoge in dein Heft. Beispiele hast du.

AAAAAA:	America / arrest / my aunt
BBBBBBB:	☺ I'm going to go to Birmingham. ☺ What are you going to do in Birmingham? ☺ I'm going to buy some boring books in Birmingham.
CCCCCC:	Cardiff / catch / cows
DDDDDD:	☺ I'm going to go to Denmark. ☺ What are you going to do in Denmark? ☺ I'm going to dance in a disco in Denmark.
EEEEEEE:	England / eat / expensive eggs

*expensive:
teuer*

4. Schreibe einige Horoskope. Die Bausteine dafür findest du unten.
Kombiniere und denke dir auch eigene Vorhersagen aus.

Jan 22 – Feb 19 Feb 20 – Mar 20 Mar 21 – Apr 20 Apr 21 – May 21 May 22 – June 21 June 22 – July 22

IDEAS FOR HOROSCOPES

You
People
There
Somebody
This week
Problems
Money

will
won't

meet somebody
help you be a lot of coming
and going
become difficult ???
? change your life
disappear ?
find new friends
be friendly get into trouble
be a problem
spend too much money
have to be careful

*change: ändern
disappear:
verschwinden
get into
trouble: Ärger
bekommen*

*careful:
vorsichtig*

July 23 – Aug 22 Aug 23 – Sep 22 Sep 23 – Oct 22 Oct 23 – Nov 21 Nov 22 – Dec 21 Dec 22 – Jan 21

Q

5. Did you know?
In den eingerahmten Infos findest du einige Angaben über das, was der durchschnittliche Amerikaner am Ende seines Lebens gemacht haben wird. Schreibe einem Freund darüber. Das Beispiel zeigt dir, wie du vorgehen könntest.

By the end of his life the average *(durchschnittliche)* American …

will have spent six months waiting at red lights.

… spend six months waiting at red lights …

… eat 87 hot dogs a year …   … drink 556 sodas a year …

… eat 5,666 fried eggs …   … enjoy 35,000 cookies …

… be to a fast food restaurant 1,811 times …

… enjoy 20 pounds of candy a year …

… walk a distance of 65,000 miles …

… eat 21.4 pounds of snack food each year …

6. Stell dir vor, dass eines Tages Astronauten auf jahrelange Weltraummissionen gehen werden. Wenn sie dann zurückkehren, werden sich viele Dinge verändert haben. Schreibe 6 bis 8 Beispiele auf. Geh dabei von den Fragen in der Box und den Beispielen aus.

> … what will have changed? … what will have disappeared?
> … what will have been invented? … what will have become a problem?
> … what will have been built?

Beispiele: *Better spaceships will have been built.*
New technologies …
Better computers …

_____

_____

_____

_____

_____

7. What will happen? What is going to happen?

Deute die Anzeichen und Angaben richtig und schreibe auf, was geschehen wird. Passende Verben findest du in den Vorgaben. Entscheide, ob du *will* oder *going to* nehmen musst.

Q

break   rain   be

burn   have   help   play

a) There are dark clouds in the sky. – *It's going to rain.* _____

b) Andy has forgotten about his pizza in the oven. – *It* _____

_____

c) There are too many books on the shelf. – *It* _____

_____

d) My sister has missed the school bus. – *She* _____

_____

e) Our neighbour is in trouble. – *I think* _____

_____

f) Oh, the ice-van is coming. – _____

_____

g) Tony is getting his tennis racket. – _____

_____

4   Relativsätze

> Du brauchst Relativsätze, wenn du etwas genauer erklären oder beschreiben möchtest. Die meisten Relativsätze werden mit **who** oder **which** eingeleitet, du kannst aber auch oft **that** stattdessen verwenden. Doch wann benötigst du welche Form? Hier kannst du es erfahren und trainieren.

Our neighbours have got three cats.
The people who live next door have got three cats.

One of their cats died last week.
The cat which ate the most (food) died last week.

Unsere Nachbarn haben drei Katzen.
Die Leute, **die nebenan wohnen**, haben drei Katzen.

Eine ihrer Katzen starb letzte Woche.
Die Katze, **die am meisten fraß**, starb letzte Woche.

1. Übertrage diese Sätze ins Englische und entscheide, ob du *who,*
which oder *that* nehmen musst.

a) Die Frau, die wir trafen, suchte ihr Fahrrad.

The woman (who / that) we met was looking for her bike.

b) Der Junge, der an der Tür steht, ist neu in unserer Klasse.

The boy _____ *is standing at the door is new.*

c) Das Auto, das du hören kannst, gehört unseren Nachbarn.

_____

gehört:
belongs to

d) Die Songs auf der CD, die ich dir geschenkt habe, sind super.

_____

geschenkt: gave

e) Die zwei Lehrerinnen, die du an der Bushaltestelle sehen kannst,
unterrichten in meiner Klasse.

_____

_____

Bushaltestelle:
bus stop
unterrichten:
teach

Wenn du bei der Person oder Sache, die du näher bestimmst, mit
wen oder **was** fragen kannst, dann kannst du im Englischen das
Relativpronomen auch weglassen. Darum die Klammer bei Satz a).

Tipp

2. Verbinde die Teile so, dass es lustige, aber nicht unmögliche
Erklärungen gibt.

A telephone is a thing …   … in which you find lots of things.

Postmen are people …   … pupils never listen to.

Keys are things …   … that rings when you are in the
bathroom.

The Internet is a system …   … that people always have to look for.

Teachers are people …   … that dogs bark at.

bark at:
anbellen

3. *Questions.* Bilde Fragen, die du für ein Quiz gebrauchen könntest.

What do you call	someone (the) people the thing an animal	who which that	drive taxis? you use for writing e-mails? come from Wales? barks? go to school to learn? helps you to listen to music? only lives in Australia?

Beispiel: *What do you call people who drive taxis? –*
You call them taxi drivers.

4. **Wie würdest du folgende Sätze auf Englisch ausdrücken?**

a) Münzen sind Dinge, die man immer braucht.

   Coins are things which (that) you / people always need.

b) War es Britney Spears, die dieses Lied sang?

   Was it Britney Spears

c) Da ist der Bus, auf den wir (gerade) warten.

   _____

d) Das war der beste Witz *(joke)*, den ich je gehört habe.

   _____

e) Unsere Nachbarn, deren Fenster in der Nacht offen waren, hatten Diebe *(thieves)* im Haus.

   _____

   _____

Tipp „Dessen" oder „deren" übersetzt du im Englischen mit *whose*.

5. Transform the underlined sentences into relative clauses. Q

a) That boy over there is my cousin. He is repairing his bike.

That boy over there who is repairing his bike is my cousin.

b) The two cats belong to our neighbours. You can see them in the garden.

_____

c) Who are those girls? They are talking to our teacher.

_____

d) Never bite the hand. It feeds you.

_____

e) This is the song. It was written by Sting.

_____

f) The world will never forget New York's famous World Trade Center. It was destroyed in September 2001.

_____

_____

destroyed: zerstört

6. Write sentences in the correct word order.

a) my / yesterday / The / cousin. / is / boy / met / you / who

The boy who you met yesterday is my cousin.

b) people / don't / always / about / like / talk / I / who / themselves.

_____

c) you / the / Do / that / joke / teacher / know / us? / our / told

_____

touch: berühren

d) that / a / don´t / you / know. / touch / Never / dog

_____

e) never / eggs / are / fresh. / I / eat / which / not

_____

5 Bedingungssätze – *if-clauses*

Willst du im Englischen über etwas sprechen, das unter einer bestimmten Bedingung geschieht oder auch nicht, dann musst du ziemlich genau auf die Formen im Haupt- und Nebensatz achten. Sonst versteht man vielleicht etwas ganz anderes als du eigentlich sagen wolltest. Also: volle Konzentration jetzt.

Fangen wir mit den **Bedingungssäzten vom Typ I** an.

MERK-BAR

Bedingungs-sätze Typ I

if-clause (simple present)	Hauptsatz *will-future*
If the weather **is** nice,	we **will go** for a walk.
If it**'s** bad,	we **won't go** out.
If you don't **take** your raincoat,	you**'ll get** wet.

1. **Füge die Teile zu sinnvollen Sätzen zusammen.**

If we take a taxi,	you'll find my e-mail.
We'll do it for them	we'll arrive earlier.
If you open your e-mail box,	we'll go for a swim.
He'll tell you	if they don't mind.
If it's warm enough,	if you ask him.

_____

_____

_____

_____

_____

Ob du nun mit dem if-Satz oder dem Hauptsatz anfängst, ist ziemlich egal. Vor *if* solltest du allerdings kein Komma setzen.

Tipp

2. **Übertrage ins Englische.**

a) Wenn es regnet, bleiben wir zu Hause.

_____

b) Wir werden uns verspäten *(be late)*, wenn wir unseren Zug verpassen.

_____

verpassen: miss

c) Wenn du diese CD anhörst *(listen to)*, wirst du viel Spaß haben.

_____

Spaß: fun

d) Ihr werdet es nicht schaffen *(make it)*, wenn ihr so langsam arbeitet.

_____

MERK-BAR

Bedingungs-
sätze Typ II

if-clause (simple past)	Hauptsatz *would*
If he **ate** healthier food,	he **would be** fitter.
If she **had** more money,	she **would live** in Sydney.

3. *If I could turn back time …*
Was würdest du alles machen, wenn du die Zeit zurückdrehen
könntest? Schreibe Sätze, dafür kannst du die vorgegebenen
Bauteile verwenden.

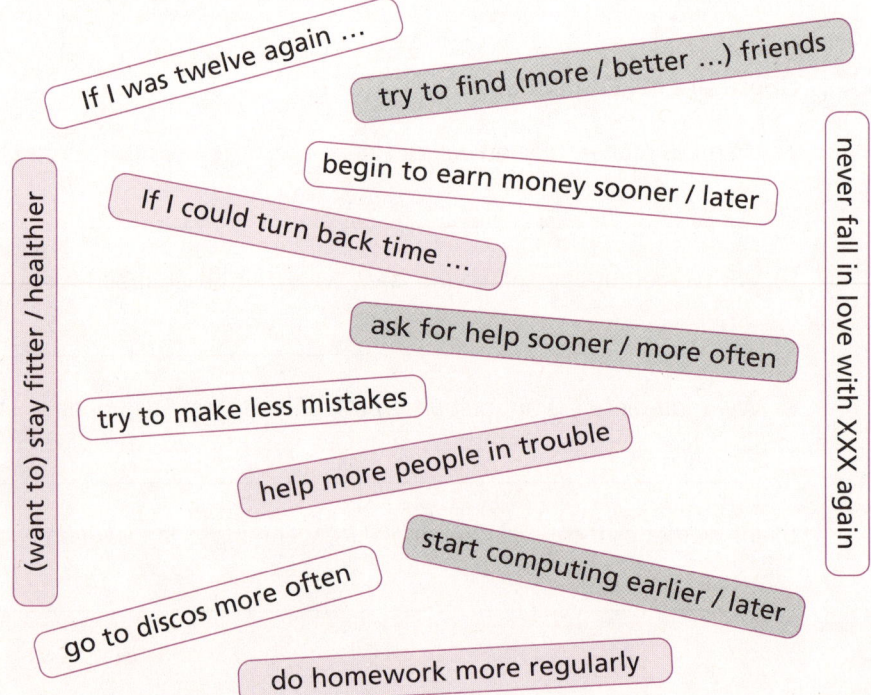

If I was twelve again …

try to find (more / better …) friends

begin to earn money sooner / later

If I could turn back time …

(want to) stay fitter / healthier

ask for help sooner / more often

never fall in love with XXX again

try to make less mistakes

help more people in trouble

start computing earlier / later

go to discos more often

do homework more regularly

Du könntest zum Beispiel solch einen Satz hinschreiben:

If I could turn back time, I would (want to) stay fitter.

4. **Sage es auf Englisch.**

a) Wenn ich mehr Geld hätte, würde ich mir einen neuen Computer kaufen.

If I had more money, I _____

_____

b) Ich würde ein Didgeridoo mitbringen, wenn ich nach Australien ginge.

_____

mitbringen: bring back

c) Wenn ich du wäre, würde ich das nicht tun.

_____

d) Was würdest du tun, wenn du ein Popstar wärest?

_____

Beim Typ II gibt es auch noch die Form *were (If I were you, …)*, doch moderner und gängiger ist die Form *was*.

Tipp

71

Q

Wenn er sich also gesünder ernährt hätte, wäre er fitter gewesen. Er hat es aber nicht getan und wird es auch nicht mehr tun können. Mit dem Typ III sprichst du über das, was gewesen wäre, wenn …. Doch weder das eine noch das andere davon ist eingetreten. Versuch's gleich selbst in der folgenden Übung.

5. Translate the missing part of the sentence.

a) _If I hadn't lost the key_____, I wouldn't have been in trouble.
(Wenn ich den Schlüssel nicht verloren hätte,)

b) If I had been more careful, _____
(wäre das nicht passiert.)

c) _____, we would have found
(Wäre er nicht zu schnell gefahren,)   the right way.

d) If you had opened your mailbox, _____
(hättest du meine E-Mail gelesen.)

e) _____, I would have known about it sooner.
(Hättest du mir davon erzählt,)

6. **Complete the sentences. Put the verbs into the right tense.**

a) I _____ you if I _____

it earlier.   **tell, know**

b) If I _____ enough money, I _____

in Florida.   **have, live**

c) If it _____ warmer, more ice _____

become, melt

d) If more ice _____, there _____ more floods.   *floods: Über-
schwemmungen*

melt, be

e) If we _____ better cycle lanes, less people _____

their cars.   **have, use**

f) What _____ you _____ if you _____

to your favourite pop group.   **say, talk**

6   Passivsätze

> Willst du darüber sprechen oder schreiben, was mit jemandem oder mit etwas passiert ist, dann brauchst du Passivsätze. Du findest sie häufig in Zeitungsberichten, Gebrauchsanleitungen oder in Protokollen. Um sie zu bilden, musst du die Wortstellung des Satzes und die Zeitform des Verbs beachten. Schau dir die Beispiele an.

*Hundreds of hurricanes **are counted** every year.*
Hunderte von Hurrikans werden jedes Jahr gezählt.

*Hundreds of people **were** badly **injured**.*
Hunderte Menschen wurden schrecklich verletzt.

Du kannst Passivsätze in allen Zeitformen verwenden – genau wie Aktivsätze. Du solltest dich aber an die **3. Form des Verbs** erinnern: *counted, injured, told, done, eaten, sold etc.*

Vergleich Aktiv *(active voice)* – Passiv *(passive voice)*

Aktiv	**Passiv**
*My dog **chased** our <u>neighbour</u>.*	*Our <u>neighbour</u> **was** **chased** by my dog.*
Mein Hund jagte unseren Nachbarn.	Unser Nachbar wurde von meinem Hund gejagt.
*The hurricane **will hit** <u>the</u> <u>south</u> <u>coast</u>.*	*The <u>south</u> <u>coast</u> **will** be **hit** by the hurricane.*
Der Wirbelsturm wird die Südküste treffen.	Die Südküste wird vom Wirbelsturm getroffen werden.

Tipp

Hast du es gemerkt? Du musst immer darauf achten, wer etwas tut oder mit wem etwas geschieht (z.B. *dog* oder *neighbour*). Dieser Teil (Subjekt) steht immer vorn. Bei *will, can, must* und *should* musst du im Passivsatz noch ein **be** einschieben *(will **be** hit)*.

1. Schreibe Passivsätze auf.

a) They count hundreds of hurricanes every year.

Hundreds of hurricanes _____

b) The hurricanes will damage lots of buildings.

_____

c) The people can't repair them easily.

_____

d) Somebody pushed my moped over.

_____

e) They stole £100,000 from the savings bank near our flat.

_____

2. Vervollständige die Sätze. Entscheide , ob du einen Passiv- oder Aktivsatz nehmen musst.

a) They _are building_____ (**build**) a new leisure centre in our town at the moment.

b) It _____ (**finish**) by the end of this summer.

c) How did the accident happen? – Well, the taxi _____ (**crash**) into the van.

d) So the van _____ (**hit**) from behind.

e) My T-shirts are clean now. Mum _____ (**wash**) them this morning.

f) And my jeans are clean, too. They _____ (**wash**) yesterday.

3. Was ist wann und wo das erste Mal gemacht worden? Bilde aus den Vorgaben richtige Passivsätze.

> + / –
> in 1489 England
> use

a) *+ and – were first used in England* _____

in 1489 (for the first time). _____

coffee bring to GB 1517	b) _____ _____
1494 distill whisky Scotland	c) *The first whisky* _____ _____
Britain 1565 pencil use	d) _____ _____
toothbrush China 1498 make	e) _____ _____
tea drink Britain 1692	f) _____ _____
England handkerchief 1503 invent	g) _____ _____
umbrella 1693 France carry around	h) _____ _____

handkerchief:
Taschentuch

umbrella:
Regenschirm

4. Raue Männer aus dem Norden. Vervollständige die Sätze.

a) In the middle of the eighth century the British Isles _____
   (invade) by the Vikings.

invade:
überfallen

guys: Kerle,
Burschen

b) These guys from Norway and Denmark _____ **(know)**
   to be taller, blonder and tougher than any other people who had
   come to Britain before.

fierce warriors:
erbitterte Krieger

c) The Vikings _____ **(fear)** as fierce warriors.

d) Hundreds of villages _____ (plunder) and

_____ (burn down) by the Vikings over the years.

e) Finally the Vikings _____ (stop) by Alfred the Great,

who was then King of Wessex.

f) Lots of place names ending with -by or -thorpe remind us of the

settlements _____ (found) by the Vikings.

remind of:
erinnern an
settlement:
Ansiedlung

5. **Say it in English.**

a) Es sind viele Bücher über New York geschrieben worden.

   Lots of books _____

b) Heute werden in New York noch immer viele Autos gestohlen.

_____

c) Wir wissen nicht, wie viele Filme über New York gemacht worden sind.

_____

d) Im Moment wird ein neues Konzept für den New York Marathon
   diskutiert.

_____

e) Diese Fotos von einem „neuen" Manhatten wurden letzte Woche
   gezeigt.

_____

f) New York wird auch der „Big Apple" genannt.

_____

Achte genau auf die Zeitformen. Wenn da steht: es sind geschrieben worden, dann musst du *present perfect* nehmen: **have been
written**. Wenn etwas im Moment geschieht, dann ist die Verlaufsform angesagt: **is being discussed**. Und wenn von der letzten
Woche die Rede ist, dann musst du *past* nehmen: **were shown**.

Tipp

Q

6.   Use the underlined words to form the passive voice.

a) Our kitchen / <u>clean</u> / every day. _____

b) Was your room / <u>tidy up</u> / yesterday? _____

c) The new by-pass road / <u>finish</u> / by next spring.

_____

d) Yesterday / Aunt Jane / <u>wake up</u> / our dog

_____

e) In how many countries / the new euro / <u>use</u>?

_____

7   Gerundium

> Die -ing-Form kennt ihr bereits. Man nutzt sie für Ereignisse, die gerade stattfinden. Mit ihr kann man aber auch aus Verben Hauptwörter machen. Das ist nicht weiter kompliziert, wenn man sich einige Vokabeln merkt, nach denen das Gerundium folgt. Schaut euch zunächst wieder die Beispiele an.

She enjoys **fishing**.	Sie mag (das) Angeln. / Sie angelt gern.
Fishing can be a nice hobby.	Angeln kann ein schönes Hobby sein.
I hate **smoking**.	Ich hasse Rauchen. / Ich kann Rauchen nicht ausstehen.
Smoking makes me sick.	Rauchen macht mich krank.
But I like **cooking**.	Aber ich mag Kochen./ Ich koche gern.

Du siehst, nach *enjoy, like* und *hate* verwendest du das Gerundium.
So einfach!

1. Wenn du zu Verben die Gerund-Form bilden willst, musst du nur noch auf die Rechtschreibung achten, wie in den folgenden Beispielen auch. Ergänze die Gerund-Formen.

Verb	Gerund	Verb	Gerund
travel	_travelling_	speak	_____
read	_____	carry	_____
swim	_____	bully	_____
ride	_____	write	_____
shop	_____	phone	_____
miss	_____	run	_____
fly	_____	drive	_____

Von der Form her erkennt man keinen Unterschied zwischen Verlaufsform und Gerund, aber von der Funktion her schon. Wenn du die -ing-Form mit einem Hauptwort übersetzen kannst, dann ist es sicher ein Gerund.

Tipp

2. Nicht alles, was auf -ing endet ist ein Gerund oder eine Verlaufsform. Finde die Wörter, die nicht in die Reihe passen, und bilde Sätze mit ihnen.

a) writing   (something)   jogging   growing

b) living   singing   darling   watching

c) morning   surfing   teaching   drinking

d) eating   dancing   Viking   playing

e) reading   flying   learning   nothing

_____

_____

_____

Q

3. Talk about what you like or don't like or even hate. Write at least three sentences in each space.

_____

_____

_____

> dancing • listening to music • cycling • I'm keen on
> • I enjoy • cooking • riding horses • I love • playing football
> • I'm good at • playing the guitar • meeting my friends

_____

_____

_____

> cleaning the kitchen • doing homework • helping my father
> • helping my mother • tidying up my room • sorting out my
> CDs • is okay for me • is no problem for me

_____

_____

_____

> I can't stand • I hate • I'm no good at • smoking
> • working in an office • answering silly questions • I'm fed up
> with • speaking English • repairing my computer

Tipp

Du kannst die Vorschläge in den Boxen verwenden, dir aber auch eigene Beispiele ausdenken: *I can't stand studying for exams. I'm fed up with revising for my exam.*

4. **Say it in English, please.**

a) Bist du gut im Laufen? _____

b) Nein, ich bin nicht gut im Laufen.

_____

c) Aber ich bin gut im Klettern.

_____

Klettern:
climbing

d) Meine Eltern mögen mein Klettern nicht.

_____

e) Und du? Magst du Schwimmen?

_____

f) Oh ja! Schwimmen ist mein Lieblingssport.

_____

Lieblingssport:
favourite sport

Zu manchen Adjektiven (Eigenschaftswörtern) gesellt sich noch ein kleines Wort dazu (Präposition): gut in etwas – *good at ... climbing / running* oder was auch immer. Und die Verneinung ist einfach *no good at ....*

Tipp

8 Indirekte Rede – *reported speech*

Wenn du berichten willst, was jemand anderes gesagt hat, dann brauchst du indirekte Rede. Im Englischen musst du dafür manchmal die Zeitformen „verschieben", manchmal ändert sich auch nichts. Auf Pronomen *(he, she, we, my, our, here, there usw.)* musst du auch achten, sonst versteht kein Mensch, was du meinst.

Sorry, I can't make it before six o'clock. I've missed the train.

It's Tess. She says she can't make it before six o'clock. She's missed the train.

Schaut euch das Beispiel genau an. Sollte die Regel noch nicht klar sein, dann stärkt euch an der Merk-Bar.

MERK-BAR

Reported speech ohne Zeitverschiebung

I'm sorry.	→	She says **she's** sorry.
I can't make it.	→	He says **he** can't make it.
We've missed **our** bus.	→	They say **they've** missed **their** bus.

Die gute Nachricht zuerst: Wenn du von der Gegenwart berichtest *(she says, he says, wants to know* usw.) musst du an den Zeiten nichts ändern. Die schlechte: Auf die Pronomen musst du immer achten *(I → he/she, we → they; my → his/her, our → their* usw.).

Tipp

Es wird Zeit für das Training:

1. **Erzähle es weiter.**

Dies sagt man dir:	**So sagst du es weiter:**
a) (sister) "I'm late."	_____
b) (grandparents) "We want to visit you all."	_____
c) (brother) "My computer doesn't work."	_____
d) (friends) "We'd like to meet you alone."	_____
e) (mother) "I don't like dad's new jeans."	_____

2. **Denis berichtet, was ihm heute schon alles so erzählt wurde. Setze die fehlenden Personalpronomen ein.**

a) Jane: I'm angry with you!   Jane says _____ angry with _____ .

b) Bill: I've bought a new   Bill says _____ bought a new

computer game for my friend.   comuputer game for _____ friend.

c) Uncle Henry: I need your and   Uncle Henry says ____ needs _____

your sister's help.   help.

d) Grandpa: Grandma and I   Grandpa says _____ and grandma

can do it for all of you.   can do it for all of _____ .

e) Fred and Tom: We'll go on a   They say _____ go on a cycling tour

cycling tour with our mountain   with _____ mountain bikes.

bikes.

Wenn du deine Einleitung mit einer Zeitform der Vergangenheit beginnst (*she said, he told* usw.), musst du eine **Zeitverschiebung** (*timeshift)* vornehmen. Schau dir die Beispiele an.

"**We can't** come."	→	They **said they couldn't** come.
"**I've seen this** film."	→	He **told us he had seen that** film.
"**I went** to Toronto last year."	→	She **told us** that **she had gone** to T. the year before.

Als Spickzettel kannst du dir Folgendes notieren:

simple present *(can't)* ⟶ simple past *(couldn't)*

present perfect *(have seen)*

⟶ past perfect *(had seen, had gone)*

simple past *(went)*

will-future *(will meet)* ⟶ conditional *(would meet)*

Wenn das alles klar ist, dann sind die Übungen ein Spaziergang für dich.

3. **Welche Äußerungen gehören zusammen?**

1 "We will welcome you here."

2 "I arrived last week."

3 "We can do it this month."

4 Fax message: "My mother is ill."

a) She phoned to say that she had lost her keys.

b) They said they would see me the next day.

c) They told me they would welcome me there.

d) She said she needed me there at her house.

5 Phone message: "I've lost my keys."

6 "We'll see you tomorrow."

7 "I need you here at my house."

e) She faxed to say that her mother was ill.

f) He said he had arrived the week before.

g) He told me that they could do it that/this month.

Neben den Zeitformen ändern sich auch solche Ausdrücke:

this ⟶ *that,* *yesterday* ⟶ *the day before*
tomorrow ⟶ *the next day*
last week ⟶ *the week before*

Tipp

4. Complete the sentences.

a) "I washed my jeans last week." (Jane)

She told me that _____

b) "We'll be late."

They said (that) _____

c) "I've read that book." (Sarah)

She said that _____

d) "He did a good job."

She remarked that _____

e) "I'm not sure." (Helen)

He told us that _____

5. Some more changes. Fill in the gaps.

here _____

last week _____ this month _____

my _____ our _____

tomorrow _____ yesterday _____

9 Modale Hilfsverben – *modal auxiliaries*

> *Can, may* und *must* brauchst du ständig. Doch musst du etwas aufpassen, weil sie einen kleinen Defekt haben (sie heißen auch *defective auxiliaries*). Sie kommen nur in wenigen Zeitformen vor, für die anderen muss man Ersatzformen bilden. Schau es dir in der Übersicht an.

	present	past	future
können	can am / is / are able to	could was / were able to	??? will be able to
nicht können	cannot / can't am not / is not / are not able to	could not / couldn't was not / were not able to	??? will not / won't be able to
dürfen	may am / is / are allowed to	??? was / were allowed to	??? will be allowed to
nicht dürfen	may not / must not am not / isn't / aren't allowed to	??? wasn't / weren't allowed to	??? won't be allowed to
müssen	must have to / has to	??? had to	??? will have to
nicht müssen nicht brauchen	needn't don't / doesn't have to	??? didn't have to	??? won't have to

1. Verbinde die Satzteile.

a) Peter can come today ——— to tell her about the bullying.

b) Yesterday I had to anwer three e-mails — but you'll find it if you look in the phone book.

c) You needn't phone him now — but tomorrow he won't be able to come.

d) We have to talk to the teacher right now — I'm 15 now and I'm not allowed out later than 10 o'clock.

e) You weren't able to find my address — and you won't have to phone him next week.

f) When my sister was 13 she was allowed out late, — and today I have to answer two e-mails.

2. Vervollständige diese Sätze mit *mustn't* oder *needn't* und einem
Verb aus der Auswahl unten.

a) My friend has broken his right arm. His teacher says

   he ___*needn't do*___ any homework.

b) We've got plenty of time. You _____

c) I must look after my purse. I _____ it.

d) My jeans aren't dirty. I _____ them today.

e) The test is difficult, but I _____ my friend's answers.

f) We can stay a bit longer. We _____ home yet.

g) Sorry, I must finish my homework. You _____ for me.

wash   go   lose   ~~do~~

hurry   look at   wait

3. *Have to / has to / had to / must?* Setze richtig ein und verwende die
Wörter aus der Box, um vollständige Sätze zu bilden.

a) Yesterday we ran out of fax paper. Dad *had to buy* _____
   some more.

b) Tom missed the school bus this morning. He _____
   to school.

c) The concert starts at seven. We _____ the
   house at six o'clock.

d) You can't pay with euros in America. You _____
   them into dollars.

e) My brother is waiting for me. I _____ now.

f) We _____ the train because it was late.

g) Klaus goes to school in England, so he _____
   school uniform.

leave

wear

wait for

walk

~~buy~~

change

go

hurry

Q

4. Mr Lazybones doesn't like working in the garden. But he has to.
What do you think? Tell him what he has to do.

drainpipe:
Regenabfluss-
rohr
mow: mähen
lawn: Rasen
weed the
garden:
Unkraut jäten
prune:
beschneiden

trim the hedge

fix the drainpipe

prune the branches

mow the lawn

weed the garden

spray the tree

oil the gate

a) Name three things Mr Lazybones has to do.

He has to spray the tree.

_____

_____

apology:
Entschuldigung

b) Mr Lazybones has lots of apologies. Write sentences with **can't** and
not able to.

Sorry, I can't spray the tree.

_____

_____

c) You are a kind person and you offer Mr Lazybones your help. Write questions with **can** or **may**.

May / Can I spray your tree? _____

_____

_____

5. You are a reporter and you have to interview the passengers of an aircraft that was hijacked. Ask questions.

a) Mussten Sie sich anschnallen? – _____
to fasten your seat-belts?

b) Durften Sie mit ihnen sprechen? – _____
to talk to them?

c) Was mussten Sie im Flugzeug tun? – _____
on the aircraft?

d) Durften Sie etwas essen oder trinken? – _____
to eat or drink anything?

e) Wie lange mussten Sie im Flugzeug bleiben? _____

_____ to stay on the aircraft?

f) Werden Sie das jemals wieder vergessen können? _____

_____ to forget it?

Diese Formen brauchst du für die Übung: *have to, could / were you allowed to, will you be able to.* Tipp

10 Adjektive und Adverbien

> Adjektive beschreiben Dinge und Personen. Sie beleben Texte und sorgen für Anschaulichkeit. Schau selbst.

1. Ein nörglerisches Gedicht

moany:
nörglerisch

grumpy: mür-
risch, brummig
bumpy:
holperig
stony: steinig

> **A moany poem**
>
> The fire's too hot and the ice is too cold.
>
> The child is too young and grandpa's too old.
>
> My mum is so friendly and my dad is so grumpy.
>
> My bike is so new and the road is so bumpy.
>
> The water's too wet and the beach is too stony.
>
> This poem's too long and I am too moany.

a) Kreise alle Adjektive ein, die du findest.

b) Gegensätze ziehen sich an, oder nicht? Finde Adjektive und ihre Gegensätze in dem Gedicht. Manchmal muss du das Gegenteil auch selbst finden.

hot	*cold*
young	_____
friendly	_____
new	_____
wet	_____
_____	_____
_____	_____

Tipp

Schau ins Wörterbuch oder in das Vokabelverzeichnis deines Lehrbuches.

Steigerung der Adjektive

sharp	sharp**er**	(the) sharp**est**
big	bi**gg**er	(the) bi**gg**est
larg**e**	larg**er**	(the) larg**est**
lonel**y**	lonel**i**er	(the) lonel**i**est

Achte auf die Rechtschreibung bei Adjektiven, die auf **-y** oder mit einem **-e** enden. Bei Wörtern wie **big, fit, hot** oder **wet** wird der Endbuchstabe bei der Steigerung verdoppelt.

 Tipp

2. Nimm die Adjektive aus dem Gedicht und trage sie in eine Liste ähnlich wie bei der Merk-Bar ein.

Grundform	Komparativ	Superlativ
hot	_____	_____
cold	_____	_____

Schreibe die Liste in dein Heft.

Kanntest du schon diese, eher seltenen Steigerungsformern:

monst	monster	(the) monstest
sist	sister	(the) sistest
teach	teacher	(the) teachest

Fallen dir noch weitere Beispiele für „ausgefallene" Steigerungsformen ein?

Lange Adjektive steigerst du nicht mit *-er* und *-est*. Wie, kannst du an der Merk-Bar erfahren.

MERK-BAR

Steigerung mit more und most

Grundform	Komparativ	Superlativ
expensive	**more** expensive	(the) **most** expensive
interesting	**more** interesting	(the) **most** interesting
famous	**more** famous	(the) **most** famous

expensive: teuer

famous: berühmt

Für welche Adjektive gilt diese Steigerungsform? – Für alle langen mit **mehr als zwei Silben** oder solche, die auf *-ing (boring)* oder *-ful (helpful)* enden. Mehr musst du dir dazu nicht merken.

3. Ergänze die Tabelle.

Grundform	Komparativ	Superlativ
dark	_____	_____
short	_____	_____
crazy	_____	_____
useful	_____	_____
funny	_____	_____
negative	_____	_____

4. Sage es auf Englisch. Sage, dass …

a) … es gestern windiger war als heute.

Yesterday it was _____

b) … Bon Jovi verrückter ist als Sting.

_____

verrückt: crazy

c) …ein schnelles Auto besser ist als ein langsames.

A fast car _____

d) …Fußball spielen interessanter ist als es sich anschauen.

Playing football _____ *than watching* ___

e) … Michael Jordan der berühmteste Basketball-Spieler aller Zeiten ist.

_____

f) …eine DVD teurer ist als ein Video Kassette.

_____

Es gibt auch einige Exoten, die völlig unregelmäßig ihre Steigerungsformen bilden: *good – better – best; bad – worse – worst*.

Tipp

Adverbien und ihre Steigerung

Adjektiv	Adverb
Sagt, wie jemand **ist**.	Sagt, wie jemand **etwas tut.**
This is an **easy** question.	I can answer it **easily**.
She's a **careful** girl.	She does everything very **carefully**.

Wenn du Adverbien bildest, musst du nur **-ly** an das Adjektiv anhängen. Dabei solltest du einige „Rechtschreibfallen" beachten: *hungry – hungrily, happy – happily, terrible – terribly.*

5. **Auf den Hund gekommen. Ergänze die Sätze.**

Adjektiv	**Adverb**
a) This dog is so **loud**.	It barks so *loudly.*_____.
b) This dog is so **stupid**.	It jumps up and down so _____
c) This dog is **terrible**.	It barks _____
d) Perhaps it is **happy**.	Perhaps it barks _____
e) Or is it **hungry**?	Does it bark _____?
f) It's not **easy** to stop it.	I can't stop it _____
g) I must be **quick**.	I must get away _____

6. **Kennst du diese Exoten? Ergänze die Sätze.**

a) Sorry I'm late. My bus came *late.*_____

b) Michael Schumacher is a fast driver. He drives his Ferrari very _____.

c) We had a really hard day because we worked very _____.

d) Your homework is good. You did it _____ this time.

Tipp

Die wenigen Ausnahmen lernst du einfach auswendig:
good – well   fast – fast   hard – hard   late – late.

Q **7.** **Schreibe auf Englisch, dass …**

a) …Gina schneller läuft als Jan.

b) …du langsamer liest als deine Schwester.

c) …euer Hund der verrückteste in der Nachbarschaft *(neighbourhood)* ist.

d) …du sehr hart für deine Abschlussprüfung *(final exam)* arbeitest.

e) …Michael Jackson am schrecklichsten *(terrible)* singt.

Tipp

Adverbien auf *-ly* steigerst du mit *more* und *most*. That's all!

11 Partizipien als Attribute

> Mit Partizipien der Gegenwart auf -ing (swimming) und der Vergangenheit (gone, done, boiled) kann man auch Nomen genauer bestimmen. Schau dir die Beispiele an.

Present participle

The ship was sinking.   Das Schiff sank gerade.
→ Everybody talked about the sinking ship.   Jeder sprach über das
                                         sinkende Schiff.

Past participle

These eggs are hard-boiled.   Diese Eier sind hart gekocht.
→ Good, I like hard-boiled eggs.   Gut, ich mag hart gekochte
                                         Eier.

1. Vervollständige die Sätze. Die deutsche Entsprechung sagt dir, worum es geht.

a) The house was   The firemen rushed to the _____
   burning.   Die Feuerwehrleute rannten zum brennenden H.

b) The girl was crying.   We talked to _____
                          Wir sprachen mit dem weinenden Mädchen.

c) The dogs are sleeping. Let _____ lie.
                          Schlafende Hunde soll man nicht wecken.

d) The bike was stolen.   He disappeared with _____
                          Er verschwand mit dem gestohlenen Fahrrad.

e) The car was damaged.   We repaired _____
                          Wir reparierten das beschädigte Auto.

2. Put these English proverbs into German.

a) Stolen waters taste sweeter.
b) A rolling stone gathers (ansetzen) no moss (Moos).
c) A penny saved is a penny earned.
d) A drowning (ertrinken) man will clutch (klammern) at a straw.
e) Don't cry over spilt (verschüttete) milk.

12 Wortstellung – *word order*

> Im Englischen musst du nicht viele Endungen lernen, dafür muss die Reihenfolge der Wörter aber stimmen, sonst versteht man etwas anderes als du sagen willst.

Zeitangabe (wann?)	Subjekt (wer, was?)	Verb	Objekt (was, wen?)	Zeitangabe (wann?
	Sandra	uses	her computer.	
Every day/ On Sundays	Sandra	uses	her computer.	
	Sandra	uses	her computer	every day / on Sundays.
	Sandra **often**	uses	her computer	on Sundays.
	Sandra **never**	uses	her computer	on Fridays.
	Sandra **sometimes**	uses	her computer	on Mondays.
On Tuesdays	Sandra **usually**	uses	her computer.	

Tipp

Du hast bestimmt gesehen, dass Zeitangaben immer am Anfang oder Ende des Satzes stehen. Zusätze wie *often, never, sometimes, always* stellst du direkt vor das Hauptverb.

1. Bringe die Informationen in Klammern an die richtige Stelle im Satz.

a) Grandma looks for her glasses. **(sometimes)**

_____

b) I feed our dog. **(every day)**

_____

c) Grandpa reads his paper. **(after breakfast)**

_____

d) My dad does the shopping. **(usually)**

_____

e) We watch the news. **(every evening)**

_____

f) We play cards. **(often)**

_____

2. **Satzsalat: Setze die Teile zu sinnvollen Sätzen zusammen.**

a) it / laughed / was / We / funny. / because / so

_____

b) go / to / wanted / swimming / was / it / We / but / raining.

_____

c) live / They / and / like / dog. / cat

_____

d) she / Is / 15 / or / 16 / old? / years

_____

3. **Complete this dialogue.**

Q

your friend: you:

a) (have / a bike?) *Have you got a bike?* _____ Yes, I have.

b) (special bike?) _____ Yes, it's a racing bike.

c) (when / get / it?) _____ I got in on my last birthday.

d) (use / a lot?) _____ Yes, almost every weekend.

e) (a good cyclist?) _____ Yes, I think so.

f) (ever / have / _____

an accident?) _____ No, never!

4. Say no!

a) He's from Chicago.

   No, he isn't from Chicago.

b) Harry's gone to the cinema.

   _____

c) We'll be late.

   _____

d) She likes Chinese food.

   _____

e) They took the bus.

   _____

f) Come here, please.

   _____

g) I could see him.

   _____

C Workshop TEXTS

1. Graffiti everywhere

Hier im Buch kannst du dich als Graffiti-Texter betätigen. Du findest einige Anfänge von Sprüchen und sollst sie richtig beenden. Vielleicht kennst du auch noch andere Sprüche, dann schreibe sie dazu.

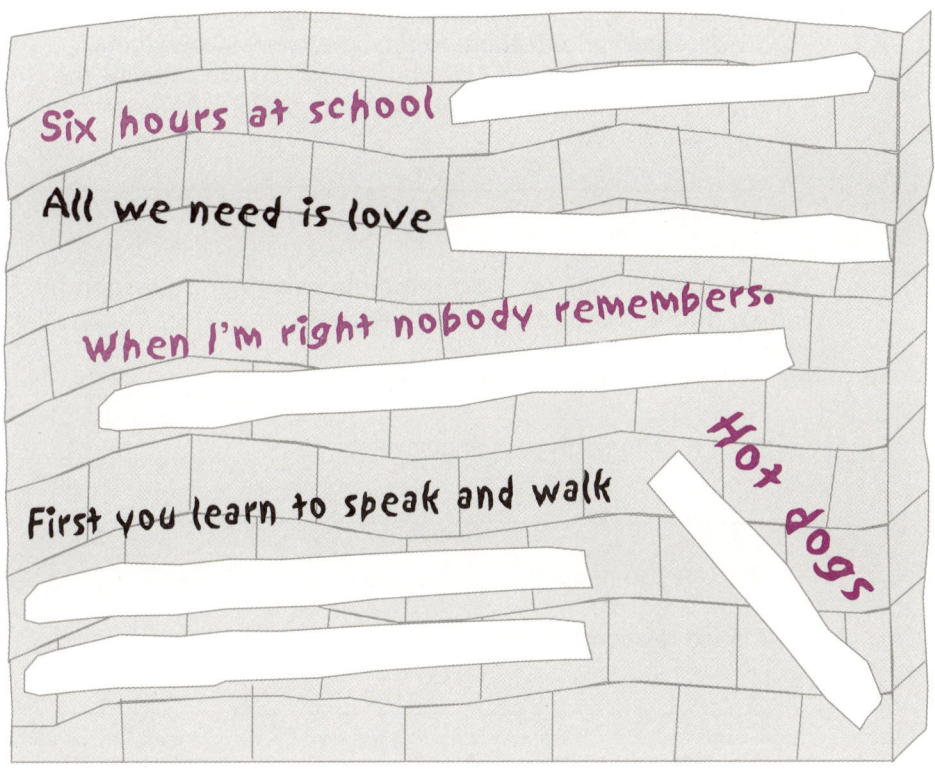

Six hours at school

All we need is love

When I'm right nobody remembers.

First you learn to speak and walk

Hot dogs

... but all we get is homework.

... don't bite.

... later they tell you to sit still and keep your mouth shut.

... is better than not sleeping at all.

... When I'm wrong nobody forgets.

2. ... like sand in your hand ...
Lies zunächst den Text durch und versuche ihn genau zu verstehen.

squeeze:
drücken

loosely: locker

possessively:
besitzergrei-
fend

> *Imagine you are sitting on the beach and you are holding fine and dry sand in your hand. If you leave your hand open, most of the sand will stay in it. But if you close your hand and squeeze to keep the sand, it will run through your fingers so that most of it will be gone.*
>
> *The same happens with a personal relationship: held loosely with respect and freedom to the other person everything will be all right. But if you close your hand too strongly, too tightly and too possessively, the relationship will slip away and will be lost.*

Wovon handelt der Text? Schreibe die einzelnen Aussagen hin, indem du die folgenden Sätze beendest.

a) You can keep the sand _____

b) But it runs through your fingers when you _____

_____

c) This can also happen _____

d) A good relationship needs _____

_____

e) But a relationship can easily slip away if you _____

_____

3. Penfriends

Laura in Boston (USA) hat ihrer deutschen Brieffreundin Svenja eine E-Mail geschrieben. Sie hat Deutsch gelernt, musste aber eine Reihe von Wörtern im Wörterbuch nachschlagen. Diese E-Mail klingt aber trotzdem komisch, oder?

```
Liebe Svenja,
Ich schreibe diese Elektronik-Post beim
Babysitzen bei unseren Nachbarn. Die Kids
schlafen schon. Die Eltern sind zu einem
Offene-Luft-Konzert gegangen. Da gibt es
Weichrock und Landmusik. Die älteren Leute
haben viel Spaß dabei. Wenn der Führungs-
sänger die Bühne betritt, dann ist das ein
richtiges Hochlicht. Ich darf den Computer
unserer Nachbarn benutzen. Meiner arbeitet
nicht. Die Heißlinie sagte, ich brauche
neue Weichware, aber vielleicht auch ein
neues Schlüsselbrett. Es ist schön, dass
ich mal wieder auf Linie gehen kann.
Schreib mir bald und bleib kühl.
Viele Grüße von deiner Laura.
```

a) Unterstreiche die Wörter, die Laura zu „wörtlich" übersetzt hat.

b) Wie müssten diese Wörter im Deutschen richtig heißen?

_____

_____

_____

_____

c) Schreibe diesen Brief so um, dass er nicht mehr komisch klingt.

4. Bad luck

Zwei deiner Freunde haben großes Pech gehabt. Nach dem Ski-Wochen-
ende sitzen sie mit einem Gipsbein da. Schreibe ihnen etwas Nettes und
vielleicht auch Lustiges auf den Gips.

with you.   Best   Get better   Be careful   mind.

You'll be   next time.   fine   soon.

Never   for you.   I feel

my symphathy.   wishes.   You have

5. Telephone notes

Was ist zu tun, wenn auf dem Telefon oder Mobiltelefon Anrufe eingehen, aber die gewünschten Gesprächspartner sind nicht da? Da sind *telephone notes* sehr hilfreich. Du hast für drei Personen Anrufe entgegengenommen und willst sie für deinen Chef festhalten. Denke dir die Namen und die Nachricht selbst aus. Du kannst dich an dem Beispiel orientieren.

Telephone Notes

Date *28/6/02*   Time *10.45*

Message for *Herrn Krüger*

From *Mr Jones, Dublin*

Message *Mr Jones is meeting you at Dublin airport an hour later than arranged.*

Taken by *Julia Roberts*

Telephone Notes

Date _____ Time _____

Message for _____

From _____

Message _____

_____

_____

_____

Taken by _____

---

date: Datum

message: Nachricht

arranged: verabredet, ausgemacht

taken by: notiert von

Telephone Notes

Date _____ Time _____

Message for _____

From _____

Message _____

_____

_____

_____

Taken by _____

Telephone Notes

Date _____ Time _____

Message for _____

From _____

Message _____

_____

_____

_____

Taken by _____

---

cancel a meeting: ein Treffen absagen, *to be ill:* krank sein, *to miss a train / plane / ferry:* Zug, Flugzeug, Fähre verpassen, *to be late:* sich verspäten

Tipp

6. **Boys and girls**

Jungs und Mädchen, da gibt es immer wieder Missverständnisse. Hast du das auch schon erlebt? Setze die passenden Teile ein.

As you looked at me _____

As you called to me _____

As you talked to me _____

As you were nice _____

As you cried _____

As you came in _____

lonely: einsam   As you were lonely _____

… But am I happy? What makes me always think of you?

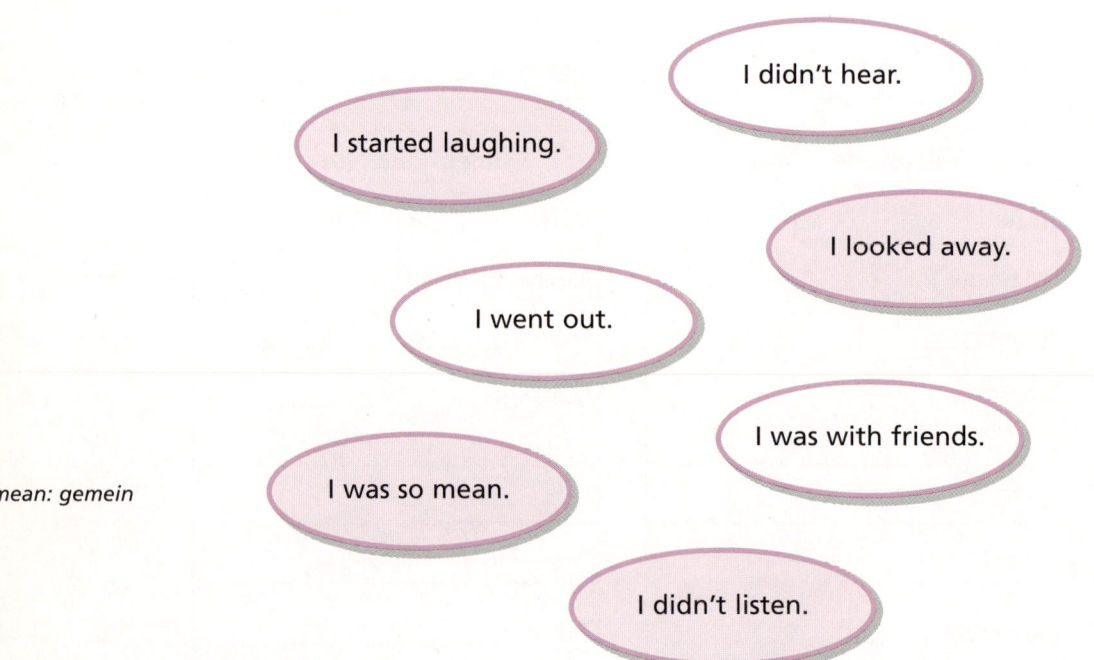

mean: gemein

7. Something was wrong

Lies zunächst diese Geschichte aufmerksam durch.

• •

One afternoon James Harrison was walking along the main street in the town centre. He was confused. He did not know where he had been before or what he was doing there. And he did not know what time it was. So he asked a woman who had come out of a shop. But the woman screamed with horror and ran back into the shop. Harrison now noticed that the people in the street were afraid of him. They backed against walls or ran across the street to get out of his way.

scream: aufschreien back against walls: sich an die Wand drücken get out of someone's way: jemandem aus dem Weg gehen

"Something must be wrong with me," James Harrison thought. "I'd better go home." He went over to the bus stop, but all the people waiting there ran away. And when the bus came, the driver did not open the doors and drove on. "Maybe somebody at home can come and pick me up," James Harrison thought. He took his mobile phone and called his wife. But the phone was answered by an unknown voice. "Is Mrs Harrison there?" he asked. "No, she isn't. She's at her husband's funeral," the voice said. "Mr Harrison was killed in a car accident three days ago."

funeral: Beerdigung accident: Unfall

• •

Beende diese Sätze für eine Zusammenfassung dieser Geschichte.

a) James Harrison was walking along a street and didn't know what time

  it was, so _____

b) The woman he asked _____

c) James Harrison noticed that the people in the street were afraid of him

  because they_____

d) He wanted to go home by bus, but _____

  _____

e) He wanted to talk to his wife on the phone _____

  _____

f) His wife was at a funeral because _____

  _____

g) Now he knew what was wrong with him. He _____

8. Don't ask a tiger!

Ergänze die passenden Zeilen in diesem ungewöhnlichen Gespräch.

I went to the zoo and asked a tiger:
Are you brown with black stripes?

stripes: Streifen

_____

And the tiger asked me:
Are you clever with stupid moments?

stupid: dumm

_____

Are you busy with lazy times?

lazy: faul
busy: fleißig

_____

Are you clean with dirty ways?

_____

Are you optimistic with pessimistic days?

_____

And he asked and asked and asked …
Better never ask a tiger about his stripes!

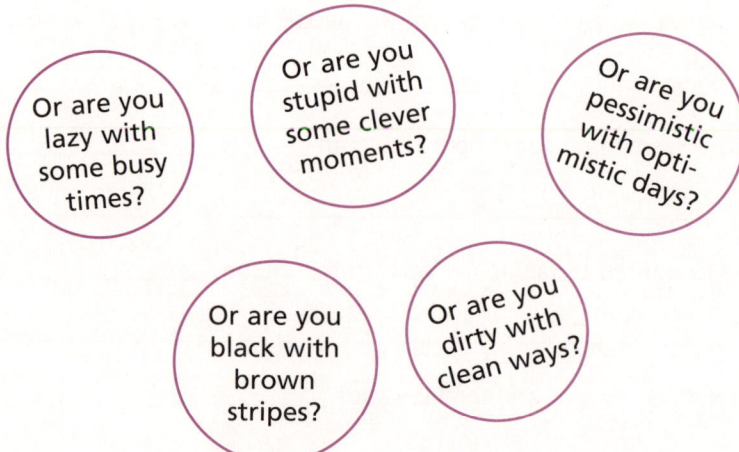

9. Teenager wisdom

Hier haben amerikanische Teenager ihre Lebenserfahrungen formuliert und ins Internet gestellt. Ergänze die Sätze sinnvoll.

a) If nothing is in the fridge _____

fridge: Kühlschrank

b) When your dad or mom slams the door when they come home

_____

slam: zuknallen

c) Don't ask your dad to help you with a Maths problem.

_____

d) Check if there is toilet paper _____

e) When you tell a lie, _____

lie: Lüge

f) When you take off your sweatshirt, _____

g) When your friends do something stupid, _____

stupid: blöde

h) Never sleep _____

i) When your mum's on a diet _____

be on a diet: eine Diät machen

j) Don't tell your teacher a dog ate your homework

_____

```
┌──────────────────────────┐        ┌──────────────────────────┐
│ before you sit down.      ├────────┤ you don't have to follow. │
└──────────────────────────┘        └──────────────────────────┘
```

follow: folgen

```
        ┌────────────────────────────────────────────┐
        │ It will turn out to be a three-hour Maths lesson. │
        └────────────────────────────────────────────┘
```

turn out: hier: sich entwickeln zu

```
┌──────────────────────┐        ┌──────────────────────────┐
│ don't eat dog food.   ├────────┤ with gum in your mouth.   │
└──────────────────────┘        └──────────────────────────┘
```

gum: Gummi, Kaugummi

```
┌────────────────────────────────┐   ┌──────────────────────────────────┐
│ it is best to stay out of their way. ├───┤ especially if you don't have a dog. │
└────────────────────────────────┘   └──────────────────────────────────┘
```

especially: besonders

```
┌──────────────────────────────────────┐
│ don't eat chocolate in front of her.   │
└──────────────────────────────────────┘

┌──────────────────────────────────┐      ┌──────────────────────────┐
│ you have to keep telling a lie.    │      │ your shirt comes up.      │
└──────────────────────────────────┘      └──────────────────────────┘
```

10. Poetry for clever people

Cinquains [sɪŋ'keɪnz] sind kleine Gedichte, die aus fünf Zeilen bestehen (*cinq* ist das französische Wort für fünf).

1. Die erste Zeile hat nur ein Wort, ein Substantiv (eine Person, ein Ort, ein Gefühl …), um das es im Gedicht gehen soll.

   ALIENS

2. Die zweite Zeile hat immer zwei Adjektive, die das Wort in Zeile 1 näher beschreiben.

   ugly: hässlich
   cruel: grausam

   ugly, cruel

3. In der dritten Zeile gibt es drei Verben auf -ing, die das erste Wort ebenfalls näher beschreiben.

   destroy:
   zerstören

   fighting, killing, destroying

4. Zeile 4 hat dann vier Wörter, die einen Satz bilden und sagen, was der Begriff in Zeile 1 so tut oder bewirkt.

   ruler: Herrscher

   want to be rulers

5. Die fünfte Zeile wiederholt mit nur einem (anderen) Wort, was die Zeile 1 aussagt. Es kann auch ein passendes Adjektiv oder Adverb sein.

   enemy: Feind

   ENEMIES

Solche *cinquains* kannst du bestimmt auch schreiben. Halte dich an das Muster, wähle Begriffe, Dinge oder Personen, über die du etwas schreiben möchtest.

_____

_____

_____

_____

_____

Tipp

Die passenden Vokabeln findest du im Vokabelverzeichnis deines Lehrbuchs oder in jedem Wörterbuch.

11. Personal poems

Hier siehst du ein Beispiel für ein so genanntes *acrostic poem* über ein Mädchen namens Christine. Das seltsame Wort *acrostic* ist mit *across* verwandt und heißt „quer herüber".

C *aring* _____

H *elpful* _____

R *esponsible* _____

I *ntelligent* _____

S *trong* _____

T *ough* _____

I *mportant* _____

N *ice* _____

E *nergetic* _____

a) Denk dir jemand aus, den du beschreiben möchtest und mache es dann wie in diesem Beispiel.

b) Solche Gedichte können sich auch um einen bestimmten Buchstaben drehen, wie in diesem Gedicht von Nora, das du vervollständigen solltst.

I'm an *N-person.* _____

Born in _____

I'm really _____

I don't like _____

I hate _____

They get on my _____

I think that's my _____

My name is NORA.

12. Writing letters

Gelegentlich muss man auch heute noch einen Brief schreiben. Besonders bei offiziellen oder formellen Schreiben muss man eine bestimmte Form wahren, wenn der Brief überhaupt ernst genommen werden soll. Hier ist ein Beispiel.

Jim Consumer
P.O. Box 67
Elk Bluff, NY 10000
February 16, 2002

Deine Adresse schreibst du oben rechts hin, darunter kommt das Datum, so oder: 16th February 2002

Customer Service
The Glades Shop
102 Marsh Street
Miami-Downtown, FLA 50000

Adresse von dem, an den du schreibst

Dear Sir or Madam,

Wenn du keinen bestimmten Namen hast, machst du es so. Sage zuerst, worum es dir geht.

complain:
sich beklagen,
beschweren

I'm writing to complain about the quality of your T-shirts.

store: Laden,
printed:
gedruckt

shrink - shrunk -
shrunk:
einlaufen

When I was visiting Miami-Downtown, I bought a T-shirt at your store. My friends thought the T-shirt was really cool. I did like the alligators printed on the front. Then I put it in the washing machine and now it's shrunk. Those alligators look like salamanders.

Erkläre dann den Zusammenhang.

grateful:
dankbar
properly: richtig

I don't want my money back, but could I have a new T-shirt, please? My size is XXL. And I would be grateful if you could send me instructions on how to wash your T-shirts properly.

Sag anschließend, was du verlangst oder dir vorstellst.

look forward
to: sich freuen
auf
receive:
erhalten

I look forward to receiving the new T-shirt from you.

Finde einen freundlichen Schluss.

Yours faithfully

Jim Consumer

Beende den Brief so, wenn du keine Person ansprichst, sonst mit *yours sincerely*.

Und jetzt du. Schreibe an diesen Laden einen Brief und beschwere dich darüber, dass die Jeans, die du dort gekauft hast, nach dem ersten Waschen völlig eingelaufen sind. Du möchtest entweder das Geld zurück oder ein neues Paar Jeans stattdessen.

_____

_____

_____

_____

_____

_____

_____

_____

Dear _____

I'm writing to _____

_____

_____

_____

_____

_____

_____

_____

_____

Hose: trousers

D Workshop TESTS

Test 1

A   LISTENING COMPREHENSION TEST

Halloween

After school had started in September, Petra was at a friend's party in Erlangen. One of the fourteen people at the party was Jim, an American exchange student. He was from Denver, and he was spending a year at Petra's school. On her way to the party Petra had seen some great Halloween decorations in a department store and decided to have her own Halloween party on October 31. So she asked Jim, "Can you tell me more about the history of Halloween? How do people celebrate Halloween in America today?"

He answered, "In the 1840s many Irish people came to America. They brought their traditions with them. One of them was Halloween. The Irish immigrants believed that Halloween was the night when the dead left their graves and tried to frighten people. To drive these spirits away, people dressed up as ghosts, witches or skeletons. They also cut terrible faces into pumpkins, lit a candle inside and put these jack-o'-lanterns in their windows.
Today American children wear costumes, too. They go from house to house shouting 'Trick or Treat', and neighbours give them some sweets.

Sometimes the kids' parents also enjoy decorating the house and celebrating Halloween. They wear funny costumes and frighten the children who come to their house asking for sweets. Others go to Halloween parties themselves. It's a funny tradition and I like to celebrate Halloween, too. By the way my grandfather is from Ireland."

"Oh, that's interesting", said Petra, "Why don't you come to my Halloween party next month?"

True or false? Make a cross.

true false

8 points
____ points

1. A friend invited Petra to a party.
2. There were fourteen people at the party.
3. Jim was from Dallas.
4. Jim was an American exchange student.
5. Petra saw some Halloween decorations in a department store.
6. Petra's Halloween party was planned for October 30.
7. Petra wanted to know more about Halloween.
8. Many Irish people came to America in the 1740s.
9. The Halloween tradition came from Ireland.
10. People were afraid of the spirits of the dead.
11. People put jack-o'-lanterns in their windows.
12. A jack-o'-lantern is a pumpkin with a candle in it.
13. Every year children go from house to house asking for money.
14. Only children celebrate Halloween in America.
15. Jim's grandfather was born in Ireland.
16. Jim asked Petra to come to his Halloween party.

Part A Total points 8   _____ points

B   LANGUAGE TEST

1.   **Find six words.**

3   points
___   points

_____   _____

_car_____   _bike_____   _____

vehicles

_ferry_____   _____

_____   _____

2.   **Find the missing words.**

4   points
___   points

Example: nurse – hospital – medicine

Job	place of work	what they work with
a) _____	office	_____
b) stewardess	_____	_____
c) _____	_____	CDs
d) _____	_____	students

114

3. **Find the other word or expression with the same meaning.**

a) twice

b) to prefer

c) sad

d) laptop

e) circle

f) autumn

1   unhappy

2   a round geometric figure

3   a small computer that can be carried easily

4   under

5   two times

6   to like something better

7   food eaten at the end of a meal

8   the third season of the year

9   difficult, hard

4. **Fill in the verb in the correct form.**

Last year Sabine and her parents _____ (be) on

holiday in Hawaii. They _____ (stay) at a nice hotel near the beach.

One day while swimming Sabine _____ (see) a big wave coming

towards her. She _____ (feel) frightened and _____ (swim) back

to the beach as fast as she _____ (can).

But today she still often _____ (think) about her holidays in Hawaii.

In two or three years she _____ (go) to Hawaii again if she has

enough money.

5. **Give short answers.**

<u>Example:</u> Do you like basketball?   Yes, I do.

a) Does your brother play tennis?   Yes, _____

b) Has your father got a new car?   No, _____

c) Will you be at home this evening?   No, _____

d) Were you at school last week?   Yes, _____

6. **Fill in the correct word.**

2 points
___ points

a) Listen! There's _____ in the kitchen.
(someone – anyone)

b) Perhaps a thief is going to steal _____.
(something – anything)

c) Is there _____ of worth in the kitchen?
(something – anything)

d) I don't think so. Oh look! There isn't _____ in the kitchen.
It's only the radio. (someone – anyone)

7. **What do you say?**

3 points
___ points

a) Schlage vor, ins Kino zu gehen.

_____

b) Bitte um Entschuldigung und frage, ob der Platz besetzt ist.

_____

c) Frage einen Touristen, woher er kommt.

_____

Points for spelling

3 points
___ points

Part B Total points 24	_____ points

C READING COMPREHENSION TEST

AUSTRALIA BY BIKE

Many people think Sydney is one of the most beautiful places on earth. Its climate is mild and there are interesting sights for example the well-known Harbour Bridge and the Opera House. Sydney attracts millions of tourists every year.

Most of them stay in Sydney, but many also travel to the outback to see Ayers Rock. Few of them, however, will see or experience Australia the way the American journalist Roff Martin Smith did. Smith had left the USA to work in Australia. He found a job with a newspaper in Sydney, got married and had two children. After more than ten years his marriage broke up, and his wife took the children with her to another town. Roff was very unhappy and wanted to do something extraordinary. He hadn't seen much of Australia, so he decided to go on a bike tour through the outback all alone.

He packed his bike with everything he needed for the journey. On June 21, 1996 he left Sydney and rode north. During the next ten months he often thought he wouldn't finish the tour. The strong winds and the hot summer sun gave him such a bad eye infection that he almost couldn't see anything for a few days. In the desert he nearly died of thirst and the heat. Another danger was the 140-ton road trains because they drove so fast on the dirt roads[1] and didn't look out for bikers. Once Roff was riding down a hill when he hit a hole in the road and fell off his bike. He hurt his shoulder and elbow and broke a few ribs. After some time in hospital he continued his trip. On his tour he met some of the best and worst people of the outback. One man wanted to smash his bike for no reason, and others didn't want to let him stay at their hotel. Most people, however, were friendly and helpful. Strangers invited him to spend a few days or sometimes even weeks in their homes when he was ill or needed help. This kind of hospitality is very important in the outback, where the nearest house, water or even tree can be two hundred kilometres away.

After ten months and 16,000 kilometres Roff arrived back in Sydney. He had lost 25 pounds during the tour, but he got to know and like Australia and its people better. However, he made up his mind to return to America, where he was born and grew up. So after nearly sixteen years in Australia and his unforgettable adventure, he went home. One of the first things he did was to write a story for a popular American magazine about his bike tour around Australia.

---

[1] dirt roads = ungeteerte Straßen

I.   **Answer the questions. Give short answers.**

5 points
___ points

1.   What was Roff Smith's job?

_____

2.   Why were the road trains a problem for him?

_____

3.   Why did he have to go to hospital?

_____

4.   What distance did he travel?

_____

5.   What did he do after he returned to the USA?

_____

II.   **Give examples from the text for the following statements. Write complete sentences.**

2 points
___ points

1.   Roff Smith met some very unfriendly people. (One example)

_____

_____

2.   Australia is a very dry country. (One example)

_____

_____

118

III. Cross out the wrong words.
Write the correct ones above.

June
Example: Roff Smith left Sydney on ~~May~~ 21.

1. Roff Smith grew up in Australia.
2. A lot of tourists who come to Australia travel by bike.
3. Roff Smith had a wife and three children in Australia.
4. He rode south when he left Sydney.
5. During his trip he got a bad ear infection.
6. He fell off his bike because he hit a stone in the road.

IV. Find the sentence with almost the same meaning.
Make a cross.

1. His marriage broke up.
   ❑ He had a nervous breakdown.
   ❑ His wife left him.
   ❑ He was happy in his marriage.

2. Hospitality is very important.
   ❑ People should be helpful to strangers.
   ❑ Good hospitals are necessary.
   ❑ Hospitals for children are important.

3. He had made up his mind to return to America.
   ❑ He didn't mind living in America.
   ❑ He minded his own business in America.
   ❑ He decided to go back to America.

Points for spelling

Part C Total points 18   _____ points

Choose **either** I. Picture Story **or** II. Letter.

D TEXT PRODUCTION

I. Picture Story

Look at the pictures and tell the story in at least 10 sentences. You can start like this:

The real driving test
One Saturday morning Nick and his father had to go shopping. Nick had just got his driving licence and wanted to drive his father's car. He asked his father, ...

II. Letter

Beachte: Dein Brief sollte mindestens 10 Sätze umfassen.
         Denke an die Briefform (Datum, Anrede, Grußformel)

Angaben zum Briefempfänger:

Deine Brieffreundin Denise Wilson (15) wohnt in Melbourne, Australien.
Sie besucht dort eine Comprehensive School. Du antwortest auf ihren
letzten Brief und gehst dabei auf folgende Punkte ein:

- Bedanke dich für den letzten Brief und den Bericht vom Ausflug in den
  Wildpark (game park). Besonders die Fotos von den Koalas haben dir
  gut gefallen, weil sie deine Lieblingstiere sind.

- Drücke die Hoffnung aus, irgendwann einmal selbst einen Koala
  berühren zu können.

- Teile mit, dass du dich auf die Australian Open freust und dass du sie
  im Fernsehen anschauen wirst.

- Bedaure, dass du nicht selbst nach Australien kommen kannst, weil der
  Flug zu teuer ist.

- Frage, für welche Wettkämpfe sie sich Eintrittskarten kaufen wird und
  ob sie für Schüler billiger sind.

- Du hast gelesen, dass Schüler während der Australian Open als
  Fremdenführer arbeiten können.
  Du fragst, ob sie an einer solchen Arbeit Interesse hat.

- Du würdest gerne ein typisches Souvenir von Australien haben und
  bittest sie, ob sie dir eines schicken würde.

- Schreibe, dass du planst, sie so bald wie möglich zu besuchen.
  Du hast bereits angefangen, Geld für den Flug nach Melbourne zu
  sparen.

- Richte Grüße an ihre Familie aus. Schreibe, dass du hoffst, bald wieder
  von ihr zu hören.

Test 2

A   LISTENING COMPREHENSION TEST

Colin's Story

One summer evening Karl was sitting in a beer garden when a young man came and sat down at his table. He introduced himself as Colin and said he was from Scotland. They began talking, and Karl told Colin something about King Ludwig and his tragic death. After their first beer Colin asked, "Would you like to hear a story which is told in the pubs about my home village near Glasgow?"
"Sure," replied Karl.

"Well, about twenty years ago the people in my little village wanted to celebrate a wine festival at the end of the summer season. A few days before the festival some villagers went to the nearest town where they borrowed a large empty barrel from the owner of a pub. Back home they put the barrel in the middle of the village square. Then they decided that each of them should pour a bottle of his best wine into the barrel. So there would be plenty of wine at the festival, they thought.
The day of the festival arrived. The women were decorating the tables at the village square when the men arrived with their bottles to fill the barrel. Only Mr McBrian, the richest man of the village, who never liked spending money without a good reason, didn't like the idea. 'I'll be very clever and I won't waste my good wine on the others,' he said to himself. 'If I pour a bottle of water in, instead of wine, no one will know the difference. There will be so much excellent wine in the barrel that no one will notice a little water in it.'
On the day of the festival everybody hurried to the square with their wine glasses. First the villagers listened to a Scottish band and danced. After some time they opened the tap of the barrel. To their surprise only water came out, because everybody in the village had had the same idea as Mr McBrian."

Karl laughed and asked, "Is it really true that you Scots are so careful about spending money?"
"Well," answered Colin, "for a long time, Scotland was a very poor country and people didn't have money to waste, but today I don't think we are any different from people anywhere else. But there are a lot of jokes like that. Do you have typical jokes about Bavarians, too?"

1. **True or false? Make a cross.**

true false

1. Karl tells Colin something about King Ludwig.
2. Colin comes from Glasgow.
3. The people in the village wanted to celebrate a beer festival.
4. They bought a big empty barrel.
5. They decided that each of them should pour a glass of wine into the barrel.
6. Mr McBrian was a very poor man.
7. Everybody brought his own wine glass to the village square.
8. The barrel was full of wine on the festival day.
9. Everyone had had the same idea as Mr McBrian.
10. Colin says there are lots of jokes about Scottish people and money.

2. **Mark the pictures of things or people that are in Colin's story.**

B LANGUAGE TEST

1. **Find two examples for each noun.**

   <u>Example:</u> parts of the body: head leg

   | 4 / ___ points |
   | 1 / ___ sp.pt. |
   | 5 / ___ total points |

   a) furniture: _____ _____

   b) computer: _____ _____

   c) illnesses: _____ _____

   d) camping equipment: _____ _____

2. **People in Britain and the USA sometimes use different words. Find the missing ones.**

   | 2 / ___ points |
   | ½ / ___ sp.pt. |
   | 2.5 / ___ total points |

car park	parking lot
holiday	_____
_____	elevator
_____	fall
flat	_____

3. *Sarah's lunch break*
   Choose the right word. Cross out the wrong ones.

   | 2 / ___ points |
   | 0 / ___ sp.pt. |
   | 2 / ___ total points |

   <u>Example:</u> ~~As soon as~~ / During / ~~While~~ her lunch break, Sarah went to a restaurant.

   a) She asked the waiter to bring her the **card / map / menu**.
   b) Then she decided to **offer / take / become** chicken and chips.
   c) Before she *left / lived / arrived* she paid the bill.
   d) Finally she walked back to work **also / although / or** it was raining.

4. **English sounds. Which word is it?**

    <u>Example:</u> ['ɪŋglɪʃ] English

    | 2 / ___ points |
    | ½ / ___sp.pt. |
    | 2.5 / ___ <br> total points |

    At the end of an enjoyable ['i:vnɪŋ] _____,

    the young ['pi:pl] _____ met at the Washington

    Monument and had a lot of [fʌn] _____ there.

    They listened to music till the next ['mɔ:nɪŋ] _____.

5. *Tony is at Sam's house.*
    Find the correct form of "be".

    | 2 / ___ points |
    | 0 / ___ sp.pt. |
    | 2 / ___ <br> total points |

    a) Tony's parents _____ on holiday in Spain at
       the moment.

    b) Tony asks, "Sam, have you ever _____ to Spain?"

    c) Sam offers Tony some pizza. Tony answers, "Thanks. I don't want

       anything to eat: I _____ not hungry."

    d) Yesterday Tony and Sam _____ at the cinema.

6. *Mary and Susan are making plans for the
    next weekend.*
    Put the parts of the sentences into the correct order.

    | 2 / ___ points |
    | ½ / ___sp.pt. |
    | 2.5 / ___ <br> total points |

    a) already / Have / for the concert / ? / bought /
       next Sunday / the tickets / you

       _____

       _____

    b) time / No, / because / have / I / haven't / didn't / I / enough /.

       _____

       _____

7. **Please compare Mary and Betty.**

Mary: 1.65 m ☹ dress: $120   maths: *has difficulties*
Betty: 1.59 m ☺ dress: $ 90   maths: *quite good*

a) (tall)   Mary is _____ Betty.

b) (happy)   Betty is _____ Mary.

c) (expensive)   Mary's dress is _____ Betty's dress.

d) (bad) Mary is _____ at maths _____ Betty.

| 3 / ___ points |
| ½ / ___ sp.pt. |
| 3.5 / ___ |
| total points |

8. **What do you say?**

a) Sage, wenn du genug Geld hättest, würdest du
dir einen neuen Computer kaufen.

_____

| 4 / ___ points |
| 1 / ___ sp.pt. |
| 5 / ___ |
| total points |

b) Du erzählst, dass ihr die Tiere im Zoo nicht füttern durftet.

_____

c) Du stellst fest, dass es heute ziemlich kalt ist.

_____

| **Part 3** Total points 25 | _____ points |

C   READING COMPREHENSION TEST

BRITAIN'S YOUNGEST INTERNET MILLIONAIRE

Tom Hadfield, 17, goes to school in Brighton, England. Last July he received more pocket money than all other Brighton teenagers together. A large newspaper company paid Tom over 100,000 pounds (€ 166,000) for his web site, 'soccer.net'. It offers soccer news from Britain and the rest of the world: the latest match results, team news and information about players.

Tom tells how he became a teenage Internet millionaire:
"I was only two when I used my first computer. It belonged to my older sister, Lucy. When I was three I taught myself how to play chess, and I often played against the computer. Of course I always lost, until I learned that I could break into the computer programme. Then I won every time. Later in school a friend introduced me to the Internet. I visited him every afternoon after school and stayed until his parents went to bed. My parents wanted me to spend more time at home, so they got me on the Internet for my 12th birthday. At first I spent up to ten hours a day on it. It was great e-mailing people around the world. They didn't know I was just a schoolboy. I began putting up soccer scores on my own homepage and started the first "live results" service on the Web.
Every Sunday my parents wondered why I ran in and out of the living room, writing down scores off the teletext pages. Then one day I was daydreaming at school when the idea for a soccer web site came to me. I worked out a plan and told my father, who is a journalist. – His newspaper let us use their soccer news reports. In August 1995 we started the web site 'soccer.net'. It has changed a lot in the past six years and has become the most popular soccer site on the Web. During the 1996 European Cup and the 1998 World Cup tournaments we had 300,000 people visiting the site every day. And still my father and I were the only people working on it.
When I'm not at my computer I play soccer for Saltdean United, a semi-professional club. I play for the under-18s, and sometimes on the first team, which travels all over England. Several nights a week, I meet my friends and we play billiards in our garage and listen to music or go into town.
I'm still only 17 and have to finish school, but I work at our London head-quarters two days a week. With the money I got for 'soccer.net', my father and I have started a new Internet business called 'School.Net'. It has teaching tips and links to the most interesting education web sites; for example, sites where you can get help with your homework. It also offers education news and information about all the schools and universities in the United Kingdom. We hope 'School.Net' will become Britain's number one education web site. It is already valued at 40 million pounds (D 66,000,000). And we've only just begun!"

I. **Answer the questions.**
     You can write short answers, too.

| 7 / ___ points |
| 1 ½ / ___ sp.pt. |
| 8.5 / ___ |
| total points |

1. How was Tom able to win chess games
    against a computer?

    _____

2. What did Tom enjoy when he started to surf the Internet?

    _____

3. What is his father's job?

    _____

4. How does Tom spend his evenings?

    _____

5. What did Tom do with the money he received?

    _____

II. **Cross out the wrong words.**
      Write the correct ones above.

| 6 / ___ points |
| ½ / ___ sp.pt. |
| 6.5 / ___ |
| total points |

Example: At first Tom spent   *10 hours* ~~20 minutes~~ a day on
                         the Internet.

1. A soccer club paid Tom 100,000 pounds for his web site.
2. Tom often played chess with his sister Lucy.
3. Soccer.net became the most expensive soccer site on the Web.
4. Many people worked on the soccer.net web site.
5. Tom plays billiards in a club.
6. He works in Brighton two days a week.

III. **Put the correct parts of the sentences together.**

3 / ___ points	
0 / ___ sp.pt.	
3 / ___	
total points	

1. Tom received more pocket money

2. Soccer.net offers

3. Tom first used a computer

4. A friend introduced Tom

5. Tom ran in and out of the living room

6. School.net has teaching tips and and links

a) to the Internet.

b) because they went to bed.

c) because he wanted to write down the soccer scores off TV.

d) the latest match results and soccer information.

e) when he was two years old.

f) to the most interesting education web sites.

g) than other Brighton teenagers.

h) to a journalist.

1	2	3	4	5	6

Part C Total points 18	_____ points

Choose **either** I. Picture Story **or** II. Letter.

D TEXT PRODUCTION

I. Picture Story

Look at the pictures and tell the story in at least 10 sentences. You can start like this:

A strange hotel

Jennifer Smith and her father flew to Houston, Texas, for two weeks. The trip to the Lyndon B. Johnson Space Center was a birthday present from her father because she was crazy about space and science fiction. During the flight ...

II. Letter

Beachte: Dein Brief sollte **mindestens** 10 Sätze umfassen.
          Denke an die Briefform (Datum, Anrede, Grußformel)

Angaben zum Briefempfänger:

Du hast vor drei Wochen Post von deiner Brieffreundin Sharon Richards erhalten. Sharon lebt in Harrow, einem Vorort von London. Da du ein großer Fan von Prince William bist, hat sie dir Berichte und Bilder aus Zeitungen und Zeitschriften geschickt.

– Entschuldige dich, dass du nicht früher antworten konntest, weil du dir den Arm gebrochen hattest.

– Bedanke dich für den Brief, die Zeitungsberichte und die Fotos von Prince William.

– Schreibe, dass es zuerst für dich nicht leicht war, die Artikel zu lesen und du oft dein Wörterbuch verwenden musstest. Aber nach einiger Zeit hast du sie verstanden und warst sehr stolz. Das Interview mit William über sein freies Jahr[1] gefiel dir gut.

– Schreibe, dass es dich überrascht hat, dass William bei einem Projekt in Südamerika mitgearbeitet hat.

– Teile mit, dass du selbst im Sommer drei Wochen lang Kinder in einem Ferienlager betreuen und dann im September eine Lehre als ... beginnen wirst.

– Frage, ob Sharon immer noch plant, im August nach Schweden zu fahren.

– Es tut dir Leid, dass ihr euch deshalb in diesem Sommer nicht treffen könnt, aber du hoffst, von ihr interessante Ansichtskarten zu erhalten.

– Richte Grüße an Sharons Freund und ihre Eltern aus und wünsche ihr viel Spaß auf ihrer Reise.

---

[1] freies Jahr = gap year

Lösungen

A Workshop WORDS

1 Laute – Buchstaben – Wörter

Seite 5 ‹

1. **blue**, true, clue, shoe, ... – **school**, **tool**, stool, fool, rule, ...
   fruit, suit, brute, flute, ... – **spoon**, soon, moon, saloon, ...
   knew, new, few, blew, threw, ...

Seite 6 ‹

2. a) two, too, through
   b) four, store, door
   c) sea, key, me
   d) goes, nose, grows
   e) bird, heard, word

3. a) **learn**, early, / **surf**, turn, burn, / **serve**, her, / **girl**, skirt, shirt, / **shore**, more, / **for**, or, short, sport / **four**, your

4. a) might, night, fight, kite, ...
   b) game, came, gain, pain, ...
   c) caught, fought, sort, ...
   d) toast, host, post, ...
   e) why, my, by, bye, fly, ...
   f) ground, found, pound, ...

Seite 7 ‹

5. a) nose, goes, hello, what, two, toast, blue, eleven, twelve,
   b) write, right, through, caught, brought, receipt, skateboard

6. My little sister Kate said, "Come on, mate, let's skate!"
   She didn't want to wait, ran straight up to the gate and didn't concentrate
   and then it was too late.
   Dear me, that's what I hate.

Seite 8 ‹

7. [nəʊ] no / know, [weə] where / wear, [njuː] new / knew, [wʌn] one / won,
   [hɪə] hear / here, [sʌn] son / sun, [raɪt] write / right, [ðeə] there / their
   (they're)

8. **go, show**, blow, hello, so, grow, no, coat, coal, phone...
   blind, buy, my, high, why, guy, fly, tie, fight...
   sound, cow, count, now, how, ground, ...
   boy, avoid, toy, toilet, boil, oil, Roy, ...
   date, rain, skate, mate, eight, train, name, ...

ear, **here**, **hear**, fear, dear, near, clear, ...
there, **fair**, hair, care, dare, fair, their, ...
tour, **sure**, poor, cure, moor, ...

9. heaven and hell / coffee and tea / a cassette with poems / that's inte-
    resting / a bottle of beer / for her or for me? / We have got an e-mail.

10. [–]: **home**, shoe, middle, canoe, tomatoes, nice, blue
    [e]: **them**, dress, get, when, leg, then, pet
    [i:]: **me**, sheep, he, tree, we, feet, she, teeth
    ❯ *Seite 9*

11. **b)** I hate to be seen.
    c) Could you wait for me?
    d) Love me tender, love me true. (Beim Tennis wird die Null als *love*
        ausgesprochen: *love fifteen* ist also 0 : 15.)
    e) Who are you waiting for?
    f) Are you empty?
    ❯ *Seite 10*

12. **lady**, city, silly, crazy, identity, body, busy, very, already
    play, say, day, may, – (pay, way, hay, ...)
    identify, my, simplify, try, buy, why

13. ... and who was looking for food in the woods almost stepped on a
    mouse. "Please, Mr Lion," cried the mouse, "don't eat me. I'd only be a
    very small meal for you!" – "You are right," said the lion, and he carefully
    stepped around the little animal – Later the same day the mouse saw the
    lion again. But now the lion was a prisoner in a net which some lion-
    hunters had hidden in the woods. With his sharp little teeth the mouse
    gnawed through the net, and the lion was free. "How can I thank you,
    little friend?" the lion asked. "Never mind," the mouse answered. "You
    let me go free earlier today, so it was my turn to let you go free."
    ❯ *Seite 11*

14. a terrible toothache / food for fitness / granny's good glasses / boring
    schoolbooks / butter and cottage cheese / a feeling for football / a silly
    rabbit / a hand-written letter

15. hut / shut, in / sin, team / steam,
    top / stop, it / sit, on / son, pill / spill,
    hop / shop, cream / scream, tall / stall, low /slow,
    tart / start, eat / seat, tick / stick, old / sold,
    and / sand, end / send, how / show, hell / shell
    ❯ *Seite 12*

2 Singular und Plural

Seite 12 ‹

1.
b) children
c) men
d) boys
e) teeth
f) countries
g) potatoes
h) women
i) buses
j) glasses
k) wives
l) tomatoes
m) rules
n) languages
o) teachers
p) feet
q) thieves
r) sheep
s) geese
t) fish

Seite 13 ‹

2. **Keine Pluralform: homework**, Biology, sunshine, information, coffee, electricity, salt, butter, wildlife, rain, oil, money
Keine Singularform: trousers, jeans, pyjamas, scissors, Physics, sunglasses, Mathematics
Beide Formen: actress / actresses, sports, houses, paths, boys, children, mice, quizes, tomatoes, clothes, stuntmen, women

3.
b) See you later alligator.
c) Thank you for not smoking.
d) Don't worry, be happy.
e) Are you laughing?
f) An eye for an eye, a tooth for a tooth.

3 Wortbildung

Seite 14 ‹

1. *-er*: manager, settler, officer, farmer, adviser
-or: doctor, director, operator, actor, visitor
-ist: cyclist, tourist, artist, optimist
-ian: Canadian, Indian, Egyptian, musician, electrician
-man/-woman: postman (–), policeman, fisherman, fireman, cameraman

Seite 15 ‹

2. *-ness*: friendliness, business, darkness, sadness, madness, emptiness, fairness, togetherness, helplessness, illness
-ing: training, cleaning, cycling, ending, computing, cooking, painting, travelling, killing, living
-ment: enjoyment, argument, agreement, settlement, treatment, development, arrangement, announcement
-(t)ion: addition, calculation, exhibition, vacation, relation, translation, operation, imitation
-(t)y: ability, identity, robbery, humanity, bakery, difficulty

Seite 16 ‹

3.
b) You can drink it, so it's *drinkable*. –
You can't drink it, so it's *undrinkable*.
c) You can forget it, so it's *forgettable*. –
You can't forget it, so it's *unforgettable*.
d) You can read it, so it's *readable*. –
You can't read it, so it's *unreadable*.

e) You can wash it, so it's *washable*. –
   You can't wash it, so it's *unwashable*.
f) You can accept it, so it's *acceptable*. –
   You can't accept it, so it's *unacceptable.*

4   Hilfreiche Abkürzungen

1.

2	3	4	5	6	7	8	9	10	11	12	13	14	15	16	17	18
h	f	l	i	e	j	k	m	n	d	c	o	b	p	a	q	r

❭ *Seite 17*

2.   body, November, nobody, city, September, baby, nasty, December, Biology, empty, grumpy, energy, identity, technology, poverty

❭ *Seite 18*

5   Präpositionen

1.   The boy is sitting **in front** *of* the TV. The dog is sleeping **behind** him. The table is **between** the armchairs. The woman is working **at** the desk. A book is **under** the chair. There are pictures **on** the walls.

❭ *Seite 19*

2.   **a)** A horse is walking **across** the road. The girl is walking **along** the road. **b)** The robber is jumping **through** the window. **c)** Some people are coming **out of** the cinema, a man is going **into** the cinema. **d)** The dog is running **behind** the cat. **e)** Two people are walking **up** the mountain, two others are running **down**.

❭ *Seite 20*

3.   **a)** at   **b)** from   **c)** at   **d)** to   **e)** up   **f)** near   **g)** along   **h)** behind

❭ *Seite 21*

4.   **a)** from   **b)** for   **c)** about   **d)** of   **e)** for   **f)** with

6   *Some* & *any* und ihre Familien

1.   **a)** some / some   **e)** any / some
         b) some   **f)** any
         c) any / some   **g)** some / any
         d) some / any

❭ *Seite 22*

2.   **a)** anything   **e)** anywhere
         b) anyone   **f)** somebody
         c) somewhere   **g)** something
         d) anything   **h)** anything / someone

❭ *Seite 23*

Seite 24 ‹

3. b) There aren't any biscuits in my lunchbox. / Es sind keine Kekse in meiner Frühstücksdose.

c) My mum hasn't got any brothers and sisters. / Meine Mutter hat keine Brüder und Schwestern.

d) I haven't got any money for this trip. / Ich habe kein Geld für diesen Ausflug.

e) Sorry, I didn't have any time to phone you yesterday. / Tut mir Leid, ich hatte gestern keine Zeit, dich anzurufen.

7 Klein, aber hilfreich: *one* und *ones*

Seite 25 ‹

1. Give me the glasses, please. / Which ones? The little ones or the big ones? / The big ones.

2. a) – The yellow *ones*. / Welche Tickets sind am billigsten? Die gelben.

b) – Yes, there is *one* over there / Gibt es eine Bushaltestelle hier in der Nähe? Ja, es gibt eine dort drüben.

c) – I like the *ones* about teachers. / Mein Vetter kennt viele Witze. Ich mag die über Lehrer.

d) – Can we have clean *ones*, please? / Diese Tassen sind schmutzig. Können wir bitte saubere haben?

e) – I think, I'll buy a new *one*. / Mein altes Fahrrad ist jetzt zu klein für mich. Ich denke, ich werde mir ein neues kaufen.

Seite 26 ‹

3. a) Could you show me the book? / Which one? The green one or the yellow one? / The green one.

b) Let's count the plates / Which ones? The big ones or the small ones? / The big ones.

c) Could you open that box? / Which one? The one on the chair or the one on the table? / The one on the chair.

d) I like that T-shirt over there. / Which one? The long one or the short one? / The long one.

8 Die Artikel: *the, a, an*

Seite 28 ‹

1. There was once **an** old watchmaker who had **a** shop in **the** centre of **a** little town. Every day **a** man stopped by and looked in **the** window before hurrying on his way.
After **a** year **the** watchmaker one day talked to **the** man and asked him why he always stopped by **the** window but never entered **the** shop. **The** man answered, "I'm **the** timekeeper of **the** town, and I have to ring **the** church bells at exactly twelve o'clock noon. So I always check with your clocks in **the** window first."
"Ah", said **the** watchmaker, "but I always set all **the** clocks when I hear **the** church bells."

2. **a)** She is a teacher.
    b) School is over.
    c) We see him three times a week.
    d) London lies on the Thames.
    e) Do you like History at school?
    f) They come from the Netherlands.
    g) Too much sugar is not good for you.
    h) What an interesting story!

9 Pronomen mit *-self / -selves*

1. **a)** myself
    b) themselves
    c) itself
    d) yourselves
    e) ourselves
    f) yourself
    g) himself
    h) herself

❯ Seite 29

2. **b)** If you can't repair your bike yourself, I can help you.
    c) Shut the door behind you.
    d) It happened on Friday.
    e) Some people talk to themselves.
    f) The women met in front of the café.
    g) Sally has changed a lot since last year.

10 Possessivpronomen klären Eigentumsverhältnisse

1. **a)** his
    b) theirs
    c) yours / mine
    d) ours
    e) Yours / Mine
    f) hers
    g) mine, his

❯ Seite 31

2. **a)** my / yours
    b) yours / mine / my / Mine / my / his / my
    c) your/ yours / my / ours (his) / theirs
    d) your / my / Hers.

3. **b)** Ist dieser Computer deiner, Cindy? Nein, es ist nicht meiner. Er gehört meinem Bruder. Meiner ist im Computer-Laden zur Reparatur. Er gab mir seinen für meine Hausaufgaben.
    d) Wo ist dein Fahrrad, Ronny? Nun, meine Schwester ist damit unterwegs. Ihres ist mal wieder kaputt.

❯ Seite 32

11   Leicht zu verwechselnde Wörter

Seite 33 ‹
1. a) Who can take Aunt Anne to the station?
    b) Please, bring your notes tomorrow.
    c) My sister has brought home her new boyfriend.
    d) Can you take this bucket to our neighbour?

Seite 34 ‹
2. a) He is wearing his new jeans.
    b) He is carrying a box of jeans.
    c) I should wear a pullover.
    d) Do we have to carry our luggage ourselves?

3. a) Her birthday is between Christmas and New Year's Eve.
    b) ... between Harry and Oliver?
    c) ... among all the boxes.
    d) The book was among the newspapers.

Seite 35 ‹
4. a) Have you done your homework?
    b) We must make plans.
    c) She has made a new start.
    d) Who is doing the cleaning today?

Seite 36 ‹
5. a) If grandma phones, tell her we are okay.
    b) When we are at the station, we must think of the tickets.
    c) I'll be at home when you come.
    d) If you want, I'll send your teacher a fax.

Seite 37 ‹
6. a) What language does this man speak?
    b) Which of the European languages do you think is easy?
    c) What is your favourite sport?
    d) Which T-shirts do you like better? The green ones or the yellow ones?

12   Unterschiede zwischen dem britischen und amerikanischen Englisch

Seite 39 ‹
1. a) BE: lorry   biscuit   lift   motorway   underground
       AE: truck   cookie   elevator   freeway   subway.
    b) BE: t**y**re   trave**ll**ing   col**ou**r   theat**re**   cent**re**   progra**mme**
       AE: tire   traveling   color   theat**er**   cent**er**   program

2. Mr Miller is a <u>headmaster (head teacher)</u>. And Mrs Miller works in a <u>shop</u>. Their two children go to school and are good <u>pupils</u>. Once a month all the Millers take the <u>underground</u> and go to the <u>cinema</u>. There they eat lots of <u>biscuits</u> and <u>sweets</u>.

138

B Workshop GRAMMAR

1 Die Vergangenheitsformen

1.

❯ Seite 43

V	W	X	Y	C	Z	S	S	A	N	G	G	F	E	D	F	O	R	G	O	T	C	B	A	W
U	B	T	T	H	R	E	W	S	D	R	Q	E	P	O	M	K	J	S	H	O	W	E	D	R
T	E	J	H	O	G	E	U	F	R	E	S	A	W	D	C	B	A	P	I	N	L	J	H	I
S	C	Z	Y	S	X	N	M	H	I	D	W	T	V	U	G	T	S	O	D	R	Z	F	W	T
T	O	O	K	E	Q	P	D	O	V	N	M	E	L	K	I	J	J	K	D	H	Y	L	V	T
R	M	R	A	N	W	R	O	T	E	G	F	N	E	D	V	C	B	E	E	A	X	O	U	E
Q	E	M	L	K	J	J	N	H	N	G	F	E	F	L	E	W	D	N	N	C	B	W	A	N
P	O	N	M	C	A	M	E	L	K	J	J	H	G	F	N	E	D	C	B	R	A	N	G	A

run – **ran** – run	become – became – **become**
ring – **rang** – rung	choose – chose – **chosen**
see – **saw** – seen	do – did – **done**
show – **showed** – shown	drive – drove – **driven**
sing – **sang** – sung	eat – ate – **eaten**
write – **wrote** – written	fly –flew – **flown**
throw – **threw** – thrown	give – gave – **given**
take – **took** – taken	hide – hid – **hidden**
hide – **hid** – hidden	speak – spoke – **spoken**
forget – **forgot** – forgotten	see – saw – **seen**
fly – **flew** – flown	swim – swam – **swum**
come – **came** – come	write – wrote – **written**

2.
b) Has Janet made her bed?
c) Has Richard taken the dogs for a walk?
d) Have your grandparents bought a new computer?
e) Has dad forgotten his password?
f) Has your sister bought a new computer game?

❯ Seite 44

3.
b) Have you faxed your teacher the homework (yet)?
c) Have you written the checklist for the basket?
d) Have you seen the film about the killer-wolves?
e) Have you heard the weather forecast?
f) Have you put grandmother's new computer game in(to) the basket?

❯ Seite 45

4.   b) ... and I have forgotten my raincoat.
         c) ... Where have you been? I have not seen you for weeks.
         d) ... Has the play started yet?
         e) ... The performance began 30 minutes ago.
         f) Grandpa came for a short visit last week.

Seite 46 ‹

5.   b) Have you ever had a virus in your software? – Yes, I have. – When did you have it? – I had it three months ago.
         c) Have you ever eaten a vegetable kebab? – Yes, I have. – When did you eat it? – I ate it last Saturday.
         d) Have you ever sung a French song? – Yes, I have. – When did you sing it? – I sang it three weeks ago.
         e) Have you ever visited Switzerland? – Yes, I have. – When did you visit it? – I visited it last year.

6.   b) were playing / started
         c) came / was repairing
         d) was not watching / phoned / was doing
         e) were leaving / stopped
         f) were painting / arrived

Seite 47 ‹

7.   b) Has Kate given the cat some milk?
         c) Has Robert found his new CDs?
         d) Have grandma and grandpa come home?
         e) Has dad taken the dogs for a walk?
         f) Have you bought the cinema tickets?
         g) Has the dog got its food?

Seite 48 ‹

8.   b) My friends haven't gone shopping.
         c) My grandpa hasn't written me an e-mail.
         d) My brother didn't take the bus.
         e) Our teacher hasn't bought this CD.
         f) I didn't do the washing-up.
         g) I couldn't hear you.

9.   b) Has your mother heard the good news?
         c) Our dad hasn't finished all the jobs in the kitchen yet.
         d) My aunt came for a visit yesterday.
         e) Our neighbours have gone to Ireland for a holiday.
         f) Poor Mrs Robins! Her old dog died last week.

Seite 49 ‹

10.   b) He has been ill for six weeks.
         c) It (all) began with a bad cold seven weeks ago.
         d) At first, the doctor didn't know which medicine would be the best for him.
         e) My grandad has been in hospital since Tuesday.

11. One day a farmer and his son **decided** to sell their horse at a village ❯ Seite 50
market, seven miles away from their home. After they had **left** the farm, a
neighbour **called** to them: "Why are you both walking when you have a
horse?" After they **had heard** this the son **rode** and the farmer **walked**
by his side. After they **had gone** on for two miles, two women **came**
along and one of them **said**: "Look at that boy. He's younger than his
father, but the old man has to walk." Then the father **rode** and the son
walked. After they **had gone** nearly halfway, two men **came** along and
said: "Why must that poor man walk? Isn't your horse strong enough
to carry you both?" So the boy **climbed** onto the horse too, and they
both **rode** on. They had been riding on for a while when some children
shouted: "Look at that poor horse. It has to carry two big men. Why
don't you carry your horse for a change? And that **was** exactly what they
did in the end. After they **had tied** the horse to a pole which they **put**
over their shoulders, they **carried** it straight into the village. The people at
the market **had never seen** anything like it before. They **laughed** about
"the farmer and his son who **tried** to please everyone."

12. Some boys were **working** in a barn near a field in Portugal. They **had** a ❯ Seite 51
dog with them, and this dog suddenly **started** barking outside. When one
of the boys **went** outside to look, he **saw** a strange"thing" with a big
head and a small body. It **looked** like a man but it **wasn't** a man. It was
standing in the middle of the field. The boy **was** afraid and **began** to
throw stones at it. But this "thing" **didn't** react. The boy **went** to touch
it, but something hit him hard. He **couldn't** see what it **was**, but it hurt
him like hell. He **ran** back into the barn, the dog after him. And from
there they all **watched** the "thing" move away in a cloud of blue light.
The next day the police **took** a photo of a large spot of burnt grass in the
middle of the field.

2   Einfache Formen und Verlaufsformen

1. **b)** It isn't raining. ❯ Seite 54
c) He hasn't been waiting for us.
d) I was sleeping when you phoned me.
e) They will arrive before nine o'clock.
f) She isn't always asking silly questions.

2. **b)** The sun was shining when we visited our grandmother.
c) What were you doing when the lights went out?
d) Did you give him his comics?
e) It will rain a bit in the evening.
f) He will be sitting at his computer when we arrive.
g) We have been waiting since six o'clock.

Seite 55 ◄

3. **b)** Yes, I go there regularly.   **e)** I had to care for her.
    c) Last week I didn't go there.   **f)** I always care for her when she is ill.
    d) My sister was ill.

4. **b)** Yes, they have.   **e)** No, I'm not.
    c) No, I haven't.   **f)** Yes, I did.
    d) Yes, they do.

Seite 56 ◄

5. This man lived in America 200 years ago. He loved life, liked to go to the pub and meet (met) friends. His wife did not like that. One fine (beautiful) morning when his wife had gone to the market, he called (for) his dog, took his gun and went hunting in the mountains. But there he felt tired and went (lay down) to sleep. – When he woke up, everything around him looked quite different. Many things had changed. The village had become larger. The people did not know him. They were wearing different clothes, too. And where his dog had gone, nobody could tell him. His house had become old and nobody lived in it any more. And so it became clear to him that he had slept for many years.

Seite 57 ◄

6. **a)** To a snowball.
    b) Fish and ships. – Wortspiel auf fish and chips
    c) With a witch watch. Wortspiel auf wrist-watch (Armbanduhr)
    d) Have you eaten anyone already?
    e) He had no body to dance with.
    f) To get to the second-hand shop.
    g) The Vampire State Building.
    h) Oh, it's you!

3   Zukunft

Seite 59 ◄

1. **B:** I'm going to write to uncle Henry.
    A: Are you going to buy a new computer game?
    A: What kind of game are you going to get?
    A: Where are you going to spend your next holiday?
    A: Are you going to visit the Kennedy Space Center?
    A: What are you going to do on Friday afternoon?
    A: How long are you going to stay there?
    A: How are you going to get to Dublin?
    A: When are you going to leave?
    A: What are you going to buy for your cousin's birthday?
    A: Is she going to have a birthday party?
    A: Are you going to paint your room?
    A: In what colour are you going to do it?

2. **b)** He is going to play football.   ❯ *Seite 60*
    c) He is going to play the guitar.
    d) She is going to wash her jeans.
    e) She is going to feed the cat.
    f) He is going to make a pizza.
    g) She is going to go shopping.
    h) She is going to phone someone.
    i) He is going to examine (untersuchen) her.
    j) He is going to ride his bike.

3. I'm going to go to America.   ❯ *Seite 61*
    What are you going to do in America?
    I'm going to arrest my aunt in America.
    I'm going to go to Cardiff.
    What are you going to do in Cardiff?
    I'm going to catch some cows in Cardiff.
    I'm going to go to England.
    What are you going to do in England?
    I'm going to eat expensive eggs in England.

4. (Vorschlag als Modell)
    There will be a lot of coming and going (this week).
    You will have to be careful. People won't be friendly.
    You won't get into trouble. Problems will disappear.

5. By the end of his life the average American will have ...   ❯ *Seite 62*
    ... eaten 87 hot dogs a year.
    ... drunk 556 sodas a year.
    ... eaten 5,666 fried eggs.
    ... enjoyed 35,000 cookies.
    ... will have been to a fast food restaurant 1,811 times.
    ... will have enjoyed 20 pounds of candy a year.
    ... will have walked a distance of 65,000 miles
    ... eaten 21.4 pounds of snack food each year.

6. (Vorschlag als Modell)
    New technologies will have been invented.
    Better computers will have been built.
    Cars will have changed. – Illnesses will have disappeared. – Finding jobs
    will have become a problem. ...

7. **b)** It will be burnt.   ❯ *Seite 63*
    c) It will break.
    d) She will be late.
    e) I think I'll help him / her.
    f) I'm going to have an ice cream. Auch möglich: I'll have an ice cream.
        Damit wird die spontane Entscheidung zum Ausdruck gebracht.
    g) He's going to play tennis.

4 Relativsätze

Seite 65 ❮

1. **b)** The boy who (that) …
   c) The car which (that) (–) you can hear belongs to our neighbours.
   d) The songs on the CD which (that) (–) I gave you are super.
   e) The two teachers who (that) (–) you can see at the bus stop teach in my class.

2. A telephone is a thing that rings when you are in the bathroom.
   Postmen are people that dogs bark at.
   Keys are things that people always have to look for.
   The Internet is a system in which you find lots of things.
   Teachers are people who (that) pupils never listen to.

Seite 66 ❮

3. What do you call the thing (which, that) you use for writing e-mails? – It's a computer.
   What do you call people who come from Wales? – They're Welsh.
   What do you call an animal that / which barks? – You call it a dog.
   What do you call people who go to school to learn? – You call them pupils.
   What do you call the thing that / which helps you to listen to music? – You call it CD-player / radio, MP3-player.
   What do you call an animal which / that only lives in Australia? – You call it a kangaroo, koala, emu, ….

4. **b)** Was it Britney Spears who (that) sang this song?
   c) There's the bus which (that) (–) we are waiting for.
   d) That was the best joke which (that) (–) I've ever heard.
   e) Our neighbours, whose window was open at night, had thieves in the house.

Seite 67 ❮

5. **b)** The two cats which (that) (–) you can see in the garden belong to our neighbours.
   c) Who are those girls who are talking to our teacher?
   d) Never bite the hand which (that) feeds you.
   e) This the song which (that) was written by Sting.
   f) The world will never forget New York's famous World Trade Center, which was destroyed in September 2001.

6. **b)** I don't like people who always talk about themselves.
   c) Do you know the joke that our teacher told us?
   d) Never touch a dog that you don't know.
   e) I never eat eggs which are not fresh.

5   Bedingungssätze – *if-clauses*

1.   If we take a taxi, we will arrive earlier.   ❯ *Seite 69*
     We'll do it for them if they don't mind.
     If you open your e-mail box, you'll find my e-mail.
     He'll tell you if you ask him.
     If it's warm enough, we'll go for a swim.

2.   **a)** If it rains, we'll stay at home.
     b) We'll be late if we miss our train.
     c) If you listen to this CD, you'll have a lot of fun.
     d) You won't make it if you work so slowly.

3.   If I was twelve again, I would begin to earn money later.   ❯ *Seite 70*
     If I could turn back time, I would try to make less mistakes.
     If I was twelve again, I would try to find better friends.
     If I was twelve again, I would start computing earlier.
     If I could turn back time, I would never fall in love with ... again.

4.   **a)** ... I would buy a new computer.   ❯ *Seite 71*
     b) If I went to Australia, I would bring back a didgeridoo.
     c) If I were you, I would not do that.
     d) What would you do if you were a pop star?

5.   **b)** ... it would not have happened.   ❯ *Seite 72*
     c) If he hadn't driven too fast, ...
     d) ... you would have read my e-mail.
     e) If you had told me about it, ...

6.   **a)** I would have told you if I had known it earlier.   ❯ *Seite 73*
     b) If I had enough money, I would live in Florida.
     c) If it became warmer, more ice would melt.
     d) If more ice melted, there would be more floods.
     e) If we had better cycle lanes, less people would use their cars.
     f) What would you say if you talked ...

6   Passivsätze

1.   **a)** ... are counted every year.   ❯ *Seite 75*
     b) Lots of buildings will be damaged by the hurricanes.
     c) They can't be repaired easily.
     d) My moped was pushed over (by somebody).
     e) £100,000 were stolen from the savings bank near our flat.

Seite 75 ❮

2. **b)** It will be finished by the end of the summer. **Achtung:** *by the end of the summer* heißt hier nicht, dass es „vom Sommerende beendet wird", sondern dass es **bis zum Sommerende** fertig sein wird. Dies ist eine Zeitangabe, nicht der *by-agent* des Passivsatzes.
    c) Well, the taxi crashed ...
    d) So the van was hit from behind.
    e) Mum has washed them this morning.
    f) They were washed yesterday.

Seite 76 ❮

3. **b)** Coffee was first brought to England in 1517.
    c) The first whisky was distilled in Scotland in 1494.
    d) The first pencils were used in Britain in 1565.
    e) The first toothbrush was made in China in 1498.
    f) The first tea was drunk in Britain in 1692.
    g) The handkerchief was invented in England in 1503.
    h) The first umbrella was carried around in France in 1693.

4. **a)** were invaded   **d)** were plundered and burnt down
    b) were known   **e)** were stopped
    c) were feared   **f)** founded

Seite 77 ❮

5. **a)** ... have been written about New York.
    b) Lots of cars are still stolen in New York today.
    c) We don't know how many films have been made about New York.
    d) At the moment a new concept for the New York marathon is being discussed.
    e) These photos of a ‚new' Manhattan were shown last week.
    f) New York is also called the ‚Big Apple'.

Seite 78 ❮

6. **a)** Our kitchen is cleaned every day.
    b) Was your room tidied up yesterday?
    c) The new by-pass road will be finished by next spring.
    d) Yesterday Aunt Jane was woken up by our dog.
    e) In how many countries is the new euro used?

7   Gerundium

Seite 79 ❮

1. travelling (traveling), reading, swimming, riding, shopping, missing, flying, speaking, carrying, bullying, writing, phoning, running, driving

2. something – darling – morning – Viking – nothing
    They came early in the **morning**. Let me tell you **something**. Will you be my **darling** tonight? **Vikings** were fierce warriors who came from the North. **Nothing** that he told me was true.

3. I'm keen on cycling. I'm good at dancing. I love cooking. I enjoy playing football. I love riding horses. I'm good at riding horses. I'm keen on listening to music.

    Helping my mother is OK for me. Cleaning the kitchen is no problem for me. Doing homework is okay for me.

    I can't stand smoking. I'm no good at working in an office. I can't stand answering silly questions. I'm no good at speaking English. I hate repairing my computer.

❭ Seite 80

4. a) Are you good at running?
    b) No, I'm no good at running.
    c) But I'm good at climbing.
    d) My parents don't like my climbing.
    e) And (what about) you? Do you like swimming?
    f) Oh yes, swimming is my favourite sport.

❭ Seite 81

8 Indirekte Rede – reported speech

1. a) She says she's late.
    b) They say they want to visit us all.
    c) He says his computer doesn't work.
    d) They say they'd like to meet me alone.
    e) She says she doesn't like dad's new jeans.

❭ Seite 83

2. a) she is / me (us)   d) he / us
    b) he's (=he has) / his   e) they'll (= they will) / their
    c) he / our

3. 1/c; 2/f; 3/g; 4/e; 5/a; 6/b; 7/d

❭ Seite 84

4. a) ... she had washed her jeans the week before.
    b) ... they would be late.
    c) ... she had read that book.
    d) ... he had done a good job.
    e) ... she was not sure.

❭ Seite 85

5. here – **there**; last week – **the week before**; my – **his / her**; tomorrow – **the next day**; this month – **that month**; our – **their**; yesterday – **the day before**

9 Modale Hilfsverben – modal auxiliaries

Seite 86 ❰

1. a) ... but tomorrow he won't be able to come.
   b) ... and today I have to answer two e-mails.
   c) ... and you won't have to phone him next week.
   d) ... to tell her about the bullying.
   e) ... but you'll find it if you look in the phone book.
   f) ... I'm 15 now and I'm not allowed out later than 10 o'clock.

Seite 87 ❰

2. b) You needn't hurry.   e) ... mustn't look at ...
   c) I mustn't lose it.   f) We needn't go home yet.
   d) I needn't wash ...   h) You needn't wait for me.

3. b) He had to walk to school.
   c) We must leave the house ...
   d) You have to change them ...
   e) I must hurry now.
   f) We had to wait for the train ...
   g) ... so he has to wear school uniform.

Seite 88 ❰

4. a) He has to fix the drainpipe. He has to trim the hedge. He has to mow the lawn. He has to prune the branches. He has do weed the garden. He has to oil the gate.
   b) Sorry, I'm not able to oil the gate.
      Sorry, I can't trim the hedge.
      Sorry, I can't fix the drainpipe.
      Sorry, I can't prune the branches.
      Sorry, I can't weed the garden.
   c) May I mow the lawn (for you)? May I weed the garden?
      May I fix the drainpipe for your? May I prune the branches for your?
      May I oil the gate for you?

Seite 89 ❰

5. a) Did you have to fasten your seat-belts?
   b) Were you allowed to talk to them?
   c) What did you have to do on the aircraft?
   d) Were you allowed to eat or drink anything?
   e) How long did you have to stay on the aircraft?
   f) Will you ever be able to forget it?

10 Adjektive und Adverbien

Seite 90 ❰

1. young / old; friendly / grumpy; new / old; wet / dry; long / short; big / small; ...

Seite 91 ❰

2. hot – hotter – (the) hottest; cold – colder – (the) coldest

3. dark – darker – (the) darkest; short – shorter – (the) shortest; crazy – ❭ Seite 92
   crazier – (the) craziest; useful – more useful – (the) most useful; funny –
   funnier – (the) funniest; negative – more negative – (the) most negative

4. a) Yesterday it was *windier* (Grundform: *windy*) than today. ❭ Seite 93
   b) Bon Jovi is *crazier* (Grundform: *crazy*) than Sting.
   c) A fast car is better than a slow one.
   d) Playing football is *more interesting* than watching it.
   e) Michael Jordan is *the most famous* basketball player of all time.
   f) A DVD is *more expensive* than a video-cassette.

5. b) stupidly   e) hungrily ❭ Seite 94
   c) terribly   f) easily
   d) happily   g) quickly

6. b) fast   c) hard   d) well

7. a) Gina runs faster than Jan.
   b) I read more slowly than my sister.
   c) Our dog is the craziest (one) in the neighbourhood.
   d) I am working very hard for my final exam.
   e) Michael Jackson sings (the) most terribly.

11 Partizipien als Attribute

1. a) The firemen rushed to the burning house. ❭ Seite 95
   b) We talked to the crying girl.
   c) Let sleeping dogs lie.
   d) He disappeared with the stolen bike.
   e) We repaired the damaged car.

2. a) Gestohlene Wasser schmecken süßer.
   b) Ein rollender Stein setzt kein Moos an.
   c) Gesparter Pfenning ist verdienter Pfenning.
   d) Ein Ertrinkender klammert sich an einen Strohhalm.
   e) Jammere nicht über verschüttete Milch.

12 Wortstellung – *word order*

1. a) Grandma **sometimes** looks for her glasses. ❭ Seite 96
   b) I feed our dog **every day. / Every day** I feed out dog. (**Zeitangaben**
      können am Anfang oder am Ende des Satzes stehen.)
   c) Grandpa reads his paper **after breakfast. / After breakfast** grandpa
      reads his paper.
   d) My dad **usually** does the shopping.
   e) We watch the news **every evening. / Every evening** we watch the news.
   f) We **often** play cards.

Seite 97 ‹

2. **a)** We laughed because it was so funny.
   b) We wanted to go swimming but it was raining.
   c) They live like cat and dog.
   d) Is she 15 or 16 years old?

3. **b)** Is it a special bike?
   c) When did you get it?
   d) Do you use it a lot?
   e) Are you a good cyclist?
   f) Have you ever had an accident?

Seite 98 ‹

4. **a)** No, he isn't from Chicago.
   b) No, Harry hasn't gone to the cinema.
   c) No, we won't be late.
   d) No, she doesn't like Chinese food.
   e) No, they didn't take the bus.
   f) No, don't come here, please.
   g) No, I couldn't see him.

C   Workshop TEXTS

Seite 99 ‹

1. Six hours at school is better than not sleeping at all.
   Sechs Stunden in der Schule ist besser als überhaupt nicht zu schlafen.
   All we need is love but all we get is homework.
   Alles, was wir brauchen, ist Liebe, aber alles, was wir bekommen, sind Hausaufgaben.
   When I'm right nobody remembers. When I'm wrong nobody forgets.
   Wenn ich recht habe, erinnert sich niemand daran. Wenn ich falsch liege, vergisst es niemand.
   First you learn to speak and walk, later they tell you to sit still and keep your mouth shut.
   Zuerst lernst du sprechen und laufen, später sagen sie dir, dass du still sitzen und deinen Mund halten sollst.
   Hot dogs don't bite.
   Hot dogs („heiße Hunde") beißen nicht.

Seite 100 ‹

2. **a)** You can keep the sand if you hold it in an open hand.
   b) But it runs through your fingers when you close your hand and squeeze to keep it.
   c) This can also happen with a personal relationship.
   d) A good relationship needs respect and freedom for the other person.
   e) But a relationship can easily slip away if you hold it too tightly, too strongly and too possessively.

3. Liebe Svenja, ❯ Seite 101
    Ich schreibe diese Elektronik-Post (= *E-Mail*) beim Babysitzen (= *Babysitten*)
    bei unseren Nachbarn. Die Kids (= *Kinder*) schlafen schon. Die Eltern sind
    zu einem Offene-Luft-Konzert (= *Open-Air-Konzert / Freiluftkonzert*)
    gegangen. Da gibt es Weichrock (= *Softrock*) und Landmusik (= *Country-
    Musik*). Die älteren Leute haben viel Spaß dabei. Wenn der
    Führungssänger (= *Leadsänger*) die Bühne betritt, dann ist das ein richtiges
    Hochlicht (= *Highlight* / Höhepunkt). Ich darf den Computer unserer
    Nachbarn benutzen. Meiner arbeitet (*doesn't work = funktioniert nicht*)
    nicht. Die Heißlinie (= *Hotline / Telefonverbindung für Notfälle*) sagte, ich
    brauche neue Weichware (= *Software*), aber vielleicht auch ein neues
    Schlüsselbrett (= *Keyboard / Tastatur*). key = *Schlüssel + Taste*). Es ist
    schön, dass ich mal wieder auf Linie (= *online*) gehen kann. Schreib mir
    bald und bleib kühl (= *cool / gelassen*).
    Viele Grüße von deiner Laura

    Liebe Svenja,
    ich schreibe diese **E-Mail** beim **Babysitten** bei unseren Nachbarn. Die
    Kinder schlafen schon. Die Eltern sind zu einem **Open-Air-Konzert**
    gegangen. Da gibt es **Softrock** und **Country-Musik**. Die älteren Leute
    haben viel Spaß dabei. Wenn der **Leadsänger** die Bühne betritt, dann ist
    das ein richtiger **Höhepunkt**. Ich darf den Computer unserer Nachbarn
    benutzen. Meiner **funktioniert** nicht. Die **Hotline** sagte, ich brauche
    neue **Software**, aber vielleicht auch eine neue **Tastatur**. Es ist schön, dass
    ich mal wieder **online** gehen kann. Schreib mir bald und bleib gelassen.
    Viele Grüße von deiner Laura

4. Best wishes. – Get better soon. – You'll be fine. – I feel for you. – Be ❯ Seite 102
    careful next time. – Never mind. – You have my sympathy.

5. *Beispiele:* Mr Y has to cancel the meeting because he is ill. ❯ Seite 103
    Mrs X is sorry to say that she'll be late because she missed her plane this
    morning.
    Mr Z would like to postpone (verschieben) the meeting until 16.00
    because his train is late.

6. As you looked at me I looked away. ❯ Seite 104
    As you called to me I didn't hear.
    As you talked to me I didn't listen.
    As you were nice I was so mean.
    As you cried I started laughing.
    As you came in I went out.
    As you were lonely I was with friends.

Seite 105 ❮ 7. **a)** ... he asked a woman who had come out of a shop.
b) ... screamed with horror and ran back into the shop.
c) ... ran away or tried to get out of his way.
d) ... the bus driver didn't open the doors and drove on.
e) ... but the phone was answered by an unknown voice.
f) ... her husband had been killed in an accident three days ago.
g) ... was dead. He was a ghost.

Seite 106 ❮ 8. Are you brown with black stripes? – Or are you black with brown stripes?
Are you clever with stupid moments? – Or are you stupid with some clever moments?
Are you busy with lazy times? – Or are you lazy with some busy times?
Are you clean with dirty ways? – Or are you dirty with clean ways?
Are you optimistic with pessimistic days? – Or are you pessimistic with optimistic days?

Seite 107 ❮ 9. **a)** If nothing is in the fridge **don't eat dog food.**
b) When your dad or mom slams the door when they come home **it is best to stay out of their way.**
c) Don't ask your dad to help you with a Maths problem. **It will turn out to be a three-hour Maths lesson.**
d) Check if there is toilet paper **before you sit down.**
e) When you tell a lie, **you have to keep telling a lie.**
f) When you take off your sweatshirt, **your shirt comes up.**
g) When your friends do something stupid, **you don't have to follow.**
h) Never sleep **with gum in your mouth.**
i) When your mum's on a diet **don't eat chocolate in front of her.**
j) Don't tell your teacher a dog ate your homework **especially if you don't have a dog.**

Seite 108 ❮ 10. Eigene Beispiele; Fehler sind hier kaum möglich.

Seite 109 ❮ 11. Born in November.
I'm really nice.
I don't like negative things.
I hate nasty people.
They get on my nerves.
I think that's my nature.
My name is NORA.

D Workshop TESTS

Test 1

A   LISTENING COMPREHENSION TEST

true	false	
X		1. A friend invited Petra to a party.
X		2. There were fourteen people at the party.
	X	3. Jim was from Dallas.
X		4. Jim was an American exchange student.
X		5. Petra saw some Halloween decorations in a department store.
	X	6. Petra's Halloween party was planned for October 30.
X		7. Petra wanted to know more about Halloween.
	X	8. Many Irish people came to America in the 1740s.
X		9. The Halloween tradition came from Ireland.
X		10. People were afraid of the spirits of the dead.
X		11. People put jack-o'-lanterns in their windows.
X		12. A jack-o'-lantern is a pumpkin with a candle in it.
	X	13. Every year children go from house to house asking for money.
	X	14. Only children celebrate Halloween in America.
X		15. Jim's grandfather was born in Ireland.
	X	16. Jim asked Petra to come to his Halloween party.

❯ Seite 113

Achtung: Erst ab 9 richtigen Antworten gibt es 1 Punkt. Und danach für jede weitere richtige Antwort einen Punkt dazu.

B   LANGUAGE TEST

1. Lösungsmöglichkeiten: van, lorry, truck, pick-up, caravan, plane, ship, bus, train, taxi, coach, motorbike, …

❯ Seite 114

2. Lösungsmöglichkeiten:
    a) *job:* secretary, manager, headmaster, office worker
       what they work with: computers, telephone, paper, fax, pencils / pens,..
    b) *place of work:* airport, plane
       what they work with: food, people, drinks, passengers, newspapers, tickets, …
    c) *job:* shop assistant, disc jockey/ DJ, musician, …
       place of work: shop/store, music shop, studio, disco, …
    d) *job:* teacher, professor
       place of work: school, university, college, high school, …

Seite 115 ❮

3. a) 5   b) 6   c) 1   d) 3   e) 2   f) 8

Jede richtige Lösung wird mit 1/2 Punkt bewertet.

4. were, stayed, saw, felt, swam, could, thinks, will go (is going to go)

5. a) Yes, he does.
    b) No, he hasn't.
    c) No, I won't.
    d) Yes, I was.

Seite 116 ❮

6. a) someone
    b) something
    c) anything
    d) anyone

7. a) Let's go
       What about going   to the cinema?
       Would you like to go
    b) Excuse me,
       Pardon (me),   is this seat taken?
       I beg your pardon,
    c) Where do you come from?
       Where are you from?

Jede richtige Lösung wird mit 1/2 Punkt bewertet. Neben den vorgeschlagenen Lösungen können auch andere richtig sein.

Für den gesamten Teil B (Language Test) werden zusätzlich 3 Punkte für Rechtschreibung vergeben. Für jeden Rechtschreibfehler wird davon 1/2 Punkt abgezogen, höchstens jedoch 3 Punkte. (Ab 7 Rechtschreibfehlern wird also kein Rechtschreibpunkt mehr abgezogen).

C   READING COMPREHENSION TEST

Der Reading Comprehension Text wird nicht vorgelesen. Für die Teile C und D darf ein zweisprachiges Wörterbuch benutzt werden.

Seite 118 ❮

I. 1. (He was) a journalist,
    2. Because they drove so fast.
       Because the drivers didn't look out for bikers.
    3. Because he had a bad accident.
       Because he hurt his shoulder and elbow and broke a few ribs,
    4. 16,000 km.
    5. He wrote an article (about his bike tour for an American magazine).

154

II. 1. One man wanted to smash his bike for no reason.
   People didn't want to let him stay at their hotel.
2. In the desert Jim nearly died of thirst.
   The nearest water can be two hundred kilometres away.

III. 1. ~~Australia~~ America   oder: ~~grew up~~ lived ❯ Seite 119
2. ~~A lot of~~   few
3. ~~three~~   two
4. ~~south~~   north
5. ~~ear~~   eye
6. ~~stone~~   hole

IV. 1. His wife left him.
2. People should be helpful to strangers,
3. He decided to go back to the USA.

Für den gesamten Teil C (Reading Comprehension Test) werden zusätzlich 2 Punkte für Rechtschreibung vergeben. Für jeden Rechtschreibfehler wird davon 1/2 Punkt abgezogen, höchstens jedoch 2 Punkte. (Ab 5 Rechtschreibfehlern wird also kein Rechtschreibpunkt mehr abgezogen).

D TEXT PRODUCTION

1. *Picture Story* ❯ Seite 120

Lösungsvorschlag:

The real driving test
One Saturday morning Nick and his father had to go shopping, Nick had just got his driving licence and wanted to drive his father's car.
He asked his father, „Can I drive your car, Dad, please?"
His father answered, „No, it's my new car!"
Nick was very disappointed.
A little later they arrived in town and parked in front of an exit next to a bank. The car blocked the exit, but Nick's father got out to get some money from the bank. He told Nick, „Move the car if somebody comes out of the exit."
He gave him the key and Nick sat in the driver's seat.
Suddenly he saw a man running out of the bank.
The man had a stocking over his head and was carrying a bag.
(Then he got into a car and drove away quickly.)
At that moment a policeman ran up to Nick's car and shouted, „Follow that car!" He jumped in and Nick drove away as fast as he could. Both cars went through a red traffic light.
Suddenly they came to a building site.

The bank robber couldn't stop his car and crashed into the fence.
Some time later the ambulance arrived and took the injured bank robber to hospital.
Then the policeman went to Nick and thanked him.
He said, „You're a great driver!"
Nick was very proud.

Seite 121 ‹

2. **Letter**

Lösungsvorschlag:

June 27, 2002

Dear Denise,

Thank you for your last letter and the report about your trip to the game park.
I especially liked the photos of the koalas because they are my favourite animals. I hope that some time I can touch a koala myself.
I'm looking forward to the Australian Open and I'm going to watch them on TV.
It's a pity that I can't come to Australia (myself), but the flight is too expensive. Which competitions will you buy tickets for?
Are there cheaper tickets for students?
I've read that students can work as (tourist) guides during the Australian Open.
Are you interested in such a job?
I'd like (to have) a typical souvenir of Australia. Would you send me one, please? I'm planning to visit you as soon as possible.
I've already started to save money for the flight to Melbourne.
Give my regards to your family.
I hope to hear from you soon.

Yours,

Test 2

A   LISTENING COMPREHENSION TEST

true	false		
X		1. Karl tells Colin something about King Ludwig.	❯ Seite 123
	X	2. Colin comes from Glasgow.	
	X	3. The people in the village wanted to celebrate a beer festival.	
	X	4. They bought a big empty barrel.	
	X	5. They decided that each of them should pour a glass of wine into the barrel.	
	X	6. Mr McBrian was a very poor man.	
X		7. Everybody brought his own wine glass to the village square.	
	X	8. The barrel was full of wine on the festival day.	
X		9. Everyone had had the same idea as Mr McBrian.	
X		10. Colin says there are lots of jokes about Scottish people and money.	

Erst ab 6 richtigen Antworten gibt es den ersten Punkt. Und dann für jede weitere richtige Antwort einen Punkt dazu.

Für jedes richtig angekreuzte Bild gibt es einen 1/2 Punkt. Für jedes falsch angekreuzte Bild wird 1/2 Punkt abgezogen. Niedrigste Punktzahl ist 0, Höchstpunktzahl ist 3 Punkte.

B   LANGUAGE TEST

Für jeden Rechtschreibfehler sowie für jede nicht ausgefüllte Lücke wird 1/2 Rechtschreibpunkt abgezogen. Es werden nicht mehr Rechtschreibpunkte abgezogen als für jede Übung vorhanden sind.

Seite 124 ‹

1. a) table, chair, sofa, cupboard, wardrobe, chest of drawers, desk ...
    b) monitor, printer, mouse, joy stick, keyboard, CD Rom, disc, Internet, ...
    c) headache, upset stomach, toothache, sore throat, flu, cold, Aids, ...
    d) sleeping bag, water bottle, torch, tent, cooker, ...

2. holiday   *vacation*
    lift   elevator
    autumn   fall
    flat   *apartment*

3. a) menu
    b) take
    c) left
    d) although

Seite 125 ‹

4. evening - people - fun - morning

5. are, been, 'm (am), were

6. a) Have you already bought tickets for the concert next Sunday?
    b) No, I haven't, because I didn't have enough time.

Seite 126 ‹

7. a) taller than   (¹/₂ Punkt)
    b) happier than   (¹/₂ Punkt)
    c) more expensive than   (1 Punkt)
    d) worse ... than   (1 Punkt)

8. a) If I had enough money I'd buy a new computer.   (1¹/₂ Punkte)
    b) We weren't allowed to feed the animals in the zoo. (1¹/₂ Punkte)
    c) It's rather / quite / fairly / pretty / cold today.   (1 Punkt)

Für jeden richtigen Satz gibt es die angegebene Punktzahl. Bei Wort- oder Grammatikfehlern wird je ein 1/2 Punkt abgezogen. Es sind auch andere Lösungen als die vorgeschlagenen möglich.

Höchstpunktzahl im Teil B: 21 Punkte + 4 Rechtschreibpunkte = 25

C   READING COMPREHENSION TEST

Der Reading Comprehension Text wird nicht vorgelesen. Für die Teile C und D
darf ein zweisprachiges Wörterbuch benutzt werden.

I.

1.	He broke into the computer programme.	(1½ Punkte)
2.	He liked/enjoyed e-mailing people around the world.	(1½ Punkte)
3.	(He is) a journalist.	(1 Punkt)
4.	He meets friends, plays billiards, listens to music or goes into town.	(1½ Punkte)
5.	He started School.Net / a new Internet business.	(1½ Punkte)

❯ Seite 128

Höchstpunktzahl: 7 + 1 1/2 Rechtschreibpunkte = 8,5

II.

1.	~~soccer club~~	newspaper company
2.	(with his) ~~sister Lucy~~	(against/with his) computer
3.	~~expensive~~	popular
4.	~~Many people~~	He and his father
5.	~~billiards/a club~~	soccer/his garage
6.	~~Brighton~~	London (headquarters)

Wird nur das falsche Wort durchgestrichen, gibt es einen 1/2 Punkt, sonst für
jede vollständige Antwort 1 Punkt.

III.

1	2	3	4	5	6
g	d	e	a	c	f

❯ Seite 129

Höchstpunktzahl für den Teil C: 18 Punkte insgesamt

D   TEXT PRODUCTION

Seite 126 ◖   1.   *Picture Story*

Lösungsvorschlag:

A strange hotel
Jennifer Smith and her father flew to Houston, Texas, for two weeks. The trip to the Lyndon B. Johnson Space Center was a birthday present from her father because she was crazy about space and science fiction.
During the flight Jennifer was reading a book / comic book / story / called "Mars Attacks" and she liked / was very interested in / was looking at / the pictures of the aliens / Mars people. After the flight they checked into / were at / the Cosmic Hotel reception desk. The woman gave Mr Smith the room key and said, "Your room is on the fourth floor." Jennifer waited at the lift / elevator. When they were standing in the lift / elevator an alien came in / got into it. Jennifer was very frightened / afraid / anxious / shocked. Jennifer's father was surprised, too. When they arrived at the 4th floor the alien left the lift / elevator. The alien carried their lugguage / baggage / suitcase and bag / to room No. 415. Jennifer's father sat in an armchair and couldn't believe his eyes / didn't say anything / was shocked. Then the alien took off his mask / helmet / and Jennifer saw it was only the hotel boy / bellboy / porter / a young man. He smiled and gave her a free ticket for the film "Mars Invasion" at the Palace Cinema. Jennifer was really happy / surprised / pleased.

Seite 131 ◖   2.   *Letter*

Lösungsvorschlag:

June 25, 2002

Dear Sharon,

Excuse me / Sorry (that) I couldn't answer sooner, because / but / I had broken / broke / my arm.
Thank you for your letter, the newspaper articles and the photos of Prince William. At first it wasn't easy for me to read the articles and I often had to use my dictionary. But after a while I could understand them, and I was very proud. I liked the interview with William about his gap year.
I was surprised that William had worked with a project in South America. This summer I'm going to look after children at a holiday camp for three weeks, (and) then I'm starting my apprenticeship as a ... in September.
Are you still planning to go to Sweden in August?
It's a pity we can't meet this summer, but I hope to get some interesting picture postcards (from you).
Give my regards to your boyfriend and your family. Have lots of fun on your trip. Yours,